The Secret Lives of Cats

Books by Vernon Coleman

The Medicine Men (1975)
Paper Doctors (1976)
Everything You Want To Know About Ageing (1976)
Stress Control (1978)
The Home Pharmacy (1980)
Aspirin or Ambulance (1980)
Face Values (1981)
Guilt (1982)
The Good Medicine Guide (1982)
Stress And Your Stomach (1983)
Bodypower (1983)
An A to Z Of Women's Problems (1984)
Bodysense (1984)
Taking Care Of Your Skin (1984)
A Guide to Child Health (1984)
Life Without Tranquillisers (1985)
Diabetes (1985)
Arthritis (1985)
Eczema and Dermatitis (1985)
The Story Of Medicine (1985, 1998)
Natural Pain Control (1986)
Mindpower (1986)
Addicts and Addictions (1986)
Dr Vernon Coleman's Guide To Alternative Medicine (1988)
Stress Management Techniques (1988)
Overcoming Stress (1988)
Know Yourself (1988)
The Health Scandal (1988)
The 20 Minute Health Check (1989)
Sex For Everyone (1989)
Mind Over Body (1989)
Eat Green Lose Weight (1990)
Why Animal Experiments Must Stop (1991)
The Drugs Myth (1992)
How To Overcome Toxic Stress (1990)
Why Doctors Do More Harm Than Good (1993)
Stress and Relaxation (1993)
Complete Guide To Sex (1993)
How to Conquer Backache (1993)
How to Conquer Arthritis (1993)

Betrayal of Trust (1994)
Know Your Drugs (1994, 1997)
Food for Thought (1994, revised edition 2000)
The Traditional Home Doctor (1994)
I Hope Your Penis Shrivels Up (1994)
People Watching (1995)
Relief from IBS (1995)
The Parent's Handbook (1995)
Oral Sex: Bad Taste And Hard To Swallow? (1995)
Why Is Pubic Hair Curly? (1995)
Men in Dresses (1996)
Power over Cancer (1996)
Crossdressing (1996)
How to Conquer Arthritis (1996)
High Blood Pressure (1996)
How To Stop Your Doctor Killing You (1996, revised edition 2003)
Fighting For Animals (1996)
Alice and Other Friends (1996)
Spiritpower (1997)
Other People's Problems (1998)
How To Publish Your Own Book (1999)
How To Relax and Overcome Stress (1999)
Animal Rights – Human Wrongs (1999)
Superbody (1999)
The 101 Sexiest, Craziest, Most Outrageous Agony Column
        Questions (and Answers) of All Time (1999)
Strange But True (2000)
Daily Inspirations (2000)
Stomach Problems: Relief At Last (2001)
How To Overcome Guilt (2001)
How To Live Longer (2001)
Sex (2001)
How To Make Money While Watching TV (2001)
We Love Cats (2002)
England Our England (2002)
Rogue Nation (2003)
People Push Bottles Up Peaceniks (2003)
The Cats' Own Annual (2003)
Confronting The Global Bully (2004)
Saving England (2004)
Why Everything Is Going To Get Worse Before It Gets Better (2004)
The Secret Lives of Cats (2004)

novels
The Village Cricket Tour (1990)
The Bilbury Chronicles (1992)
Bilbury Grange (1993)
Mrs Caldicot's Cabbage War (1993)
Bilbury Revels (1994)
Deadline (1994)
The Man Who Inherited a Golf Course (1995)
Bilbury Country (1996)
Second Innings (1999)
Around the Wicket (2000)
It's Never Too Late (2001)
Paris In My Springtime (2002)
Mrs Caldicot's Knickerbocker Glory (2003)

short stories
Bilbury Pie (1995)

on cricket
Thomas Winsden's Cricketing Almanack (1983)
Diary Of A Cricket Lover (1984)

as Edward Vernon
Practice Makes Perfect (1977)
Practise What You Preach (1978)
Getting Into Practice (1979)
Aphrodisiacs – An Owner's Manual (1983)
The Complete Guide To Life (1984)

as Marc Charbonnier
Tunnel (novel 1980)

with Alice
Alice's Diary (1989)
Alice's Adventures (1992)

with Dr Alan C Turin
No More Headaches (1981)

With Donna Antoinette Coleman
How To Conquer Health Problems Between Ages 50 and 120 (2003)

The Secret Lives of Cats

Vernon Coleman

With illustrations by the author

Chilton Designs

Published by Chilton Designs, Publishing House, Trinity Place, Barnstaple, Devon EX32 9HG, England

ISBN: 1 898146 70 5

Note
All characters, organisations, businesses and places in this book are fictitious, and any resemblance to real persons (living or dead), organisations, businesses or places is purely coincidental.

A catalogue record for this book is available from the British Library.

Printed and bound in the UK by J.W. Arrowsmith Ltd., Bristol

Dedication

To Donna Antoinette, a princess among cat lovers, an Upright for whom a glimpse of a cat is a glimpse of a better, more beautiful world. She knows that the better world which awaits us all most certainly contains cats.

Foreword

The Secret Lives Of Cats consists of selected letters between two cats: Lemon-Coloured Lion Heart With Long Fine Whiskers and his mother (known here as Maman).

These 'letters' were selected and abridged from an archived correspondence which took place over several years. Since both cats communicated with one another on a daily basis (on some days they communicated with one another a dozen or more times) and since it is possible for cats to have lengthy exchanges with one another it should be clear that what appears here is only a tiny fraction of the total number of words available.

The book begins with a 'letter' which Lemon-Coloured Lion Heart With Long Fine Whiskers sent to his mother when the two cats were first separated. The rest of the book consists of a selection of the subsequent 'letters' which were exchanged between the two cats and are, I believe, an accurate and revealing record of the developing relationship between a loving and caring mother and her maturing kitten. For reasons of space not all the correspondence between the two cats is included here and occasionally, where it seemed more appropriate, several letters from one cat to the other may be included in a row (with the intervening replies omitted).

Vernon Coleman July 2004

Preface

Cats don't write letters, of course. By that I mean that they don't take a pen and a piece of paper, jot down their thoughts, fears, news and dreams, fold the paper, put it into an envelope, seal the envelope, add an address and a stamp and then put the resultant slim packet into a post box. They don't bother with this rather clumsy form of communication because they don't have to. Cats can, and do, communicate with one another (and can do so over long distances) but they don't need to do so by sending one another letters. They don't use the telephone, the fax machine or e-mail either. To cats, all these forms of communication are clumsy, slow and (important for a species which takes its privacy very seriously) lacking in confidentiality.

So, how do they do it?

Simple.

Cats communicate with one another using their own effective, efficient form of telepathy.

Many Uprights have, for a number of years, been aware of the possibility of communicating with one another by telepathy. The scientific literature is full of articles by learned Upright experts exploring the ways in which men and women might be able to send and receive messages using only their minds. What none of these learned authors seem to be aware of is that cats have been using their very own version of telepathy for centuries. I discovered the existence of this communication system recently while conducting my researches into the cat world and have given the communication system the name 'felipathy'.

When cats merely appear to be sleeping (and many cat lovers, naturally unaware of the phenomenon of felipathy, have often expressed innocent astonishment at the amount of time cats spend sleeping) they are, in fact, frequently busy sending and receiving messages to other cats. The twitches and involuntary movements which can often be observed among sleeping cats – and which are usually and erroneously dismissed as merely signs that Smoky or Lemon-Coloured Lion Heart With Long Fine Whiskers is busy 'chasing rabbits' – are simply signs that Smoky or Lemon-Coloured Lion Heart With Long Fine Whiskers is, in fact, engaged in an unusually hectic and, perhaps, emotionally charged conversation with another cat or (and cats using felipathy often use what we would call 'conference calls') several other cats.

Up until now no Upright has ever been allowed access to the private correspondence exchanged by cats communicating with one another through felipathy.

Cats have published written material of course. I myself helped Alice publish her best-selling books *Alice's Diary* and *Alice's Adventures* and I have been privileged to help edit and publish poetry and prose written by a number of other cats (*The Cats' Own Annual* contains good examples of writing by cats).

But, up until now, cats have always been very careful to protect the privacy of genuine letters exchanged through the medium of felipathy. It has been generally thought, by cats everywhere, that allowing Uprights to have access to material exchanged in this way would be a reckless and irresponsible breach of privacy and confidentiality – those qualities which are valued so highly by members of the wider feline community.

I was, therefore, extremely honoured when I was chosen to edit and publish the volume of private letters which you are now holding.

When I was first approached and asked to prepare this book I had two questions: 'How do I (and my readers) know that this material is genuine?' and 'Why have you decided to allow me to publish this correspondence now?'

The answers to both questions were simple and straightforward.

'Readers who understand anything at all about cats will

immediately recognise the veracity and genuine nature of this correspondence,' was the reply to my first question. 'We realise that there will be some doubters. But this does not concern us. Those who love cats, and who have open and receptive minds, will believe, understand and learn.'

In answer to my second question I was told that a felipathic survey of cats had shown a widespread enthusiasm for rewarding cat lovers with some genuine insight into the way cats think and communicate with one another.

'There are many myths about cats,' I was told. 'We think that the time is now right for us to share another aspect of our lives with Uprights.'

I am, of course, extremely honoured to have been given this opportunity to introduce cat lovers around the world to the secret lives of cats.

Vernon Coleman July 2004

P.S. The drawings with which this volume is illustrated are entirely my own responsibility. I asked for (and am grateful to have been granted) permission to add these illustrations to this book. I would, however, like to make it clear that neither of the cats responsible for the 'letters' in this book were in any way involved in the production or selection of the illustrations.

P.P.S. Cats respond to the names we Uprights give them, and they are always happy for us to refer to them by those names, but when addressing one another they usually prefer to use their proper names; these being far more beautiful than the names we tend to give them and always being given to cats by their mothers when they reach the age of six weeks. Up until that point all young cats are known simply as 'kitten'.

The names mother cats give their kittens are always carefully considered and appropriate and have more in common with the names Native American Indians give their children than the names we choose for cats.

'It is only with the heart that one can see rightly; what is essential is invisible to the eye.'
ANTOINE DE SAINT EXUPERY

The Secret Lives of Cats

Dear Maman

I have been away from you and the rest of the family for less than two hours but it seems like two years. I miss you so much; and although I am determined to be brave and to be a credit to you I cannot hide from you the fact that I feel overwhelmed with a great sadness and apprehension. I feel some anger too, towards the Uprights who gave me away. How could the Upright with the Curly Red Hair and the Upright Who Smokes a Pipe do that? I know you had tried to prepare all of us for what you knew would happen but I never really believed that what you said would happen would actually happen to me.

When the New Uprights visited and started to make a fuss of us all I realised at once what was happening. At first I tried to look quiet and unattractive so that they wouldn't choose me to take with them. But (and I now feel ashamed of this) it wasn't long before I succumbed to the temptation to play and have some fun and show them what a jolly fellow I can be. I really, really hate to admit this but I am afraid that I think I wanted to impress them. I was showing off.

Why did this have to happen? Why are Uprights so cruel?

Your loving kitten

Lemon-Coloured Lion Heart With Long Fine Whiskers

Dear Lemon-Coloured Lion Heart With Long Fine Whiskers

You are not alone, and never will be. And you must never blame our Uprights for sending you away. They are not bad people and they did only what they thought they had to do. They were broken hearted after you had left. There were many tears from the Upright with the Curly Red Hair, and the Upright Who Smokes a Pipe banged around in the garage for several hours after you had gone.

When you were born I knew that you and I would only have a few weeks together. But although it saddened me to know that you would inevitably be taken from me, I was comforted by the knowledge that however great the physical distance between us might become you and I would always be able to stay in touch with one another. You should feel sorry for the Uprights. They are unable to communicate with each other through their minds and, when separated from their loved ones, can only communicate using clumsy methods which rely on machines. The poor dears think that using their computers to send e-mails to one another is modern and sophisticated whereas in reality, of course, it is no more sophisticated or advanced than the telephone or the fax machine. And it is, of course, far slower, far less reliable and far less private than felipathy.

You must always remember, my dear Lemon-Coloured Lion Heart With Long Fine Whiskers, that when the great Cat God created us his Plan was subtle, wise and sophisticated. You will hear it said by some Uprights that, in the beginning, God created Uprights, but seeing him so feeble, He gave him the cat. That claim, although admittedly self-effacing, assumes, with perhaps pardonable arrogance, that it was the Upright who was created first. The truth is that God gave us Uprights as our servants, to protect and serve us, and it was only after that disastrous fateful moment in the Garden of Butterflies, when our great ancestor, Marmalade the First, fell to temptation and ate the forbidden Cabbage White, that the Great Cat God allowed Uprights freedom of will and gave us the responsibility of re-establishing our natural and (originally) God given supremacy over them.

No one knows an Upright as well as the cat who lives with him or her. Even Uprights acknowledge the truth of this. I once overheard a very clever Upright telling another Upright that if he wanted to know the real character of a man he should first find out what his cat thought of him.

Our task as cats is to use this understanding to help us to educate Uprights, to lead them away from the path of indignant and false moral righteousness which some of their leaders have mistakenly chosen for them and to lead them instead back towards peaceful, loving coexistence. Uprights who think they are great sometimes have a tendency to make other Uprights (and cats too) feel small and insignificant. But genuinely great Uprights have the ability to make all Uprights (and all cats) feel great and significant.

It is our responsibility to show them, through example, the values and virtues which we have found most rewarding and most conducive to a long, peaceful and rewarding life. It is part of our job to make our own Uprights feel special. An Upright who lives with a cat should never again feel lonely, abandoned or unloved. These days Uprights have less time to do more and more. It is our responsibility to show them how it is still possible to have a fulfilling life, how they can spread more over less and make it appear, both to themselves and to others, that they are spreading less over more.

Although Uprights were originally designed, and therefore destined, to be our servants your father and I (and many other cats with whom we have both communicated) believe that no species should take, or aspire to take, superiority over any other species. Equality should be our aim – not superiority. We believe that only when Uprights recognise the truth of this will they be able to live in peace and harmony with other species and with themselves. The bigotry and prejudices which inspire violence and which are used to excuse greed and envy will be vanquished when Uprights accept the validity and natural justice of this philosophy.

And that, dear Lemon-Coloured Lion Heart With Long Fine Whiskers, is why you are now find yourself living with new Uprights. You, like your brothers and sisters, have a great responsibility. It is your mission to captivate your adopted Uprights, to soften their hearts and to capture their minds; to prepare them to receive the truth.

You will find some Uprights more difficult to train than others. Uprights are a rather mysterious breed. Uprights possess so many of the same qualities as some cats that it is sometimes hard to tell the cats and the Uprights apart but I sometimes feel that there is less going on in their minds than we suspect.

Don't make the mistake of underestimating the intelligence of

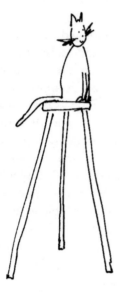

It is our task to educate Uprights.

Uprights. As the great La Nureyev once said: 'The intelligence of Uprights can be placed well above that of dogs and uncomfortably close to that of cats.'

Be endearing, my Lemon-Coloured Lion Heart With Long Fine Whiskers. Love will eventually conquer all. I have noticed that what Uprights most appreciate in a cat is our ability to offer friendship when friendship is needed, companionship when companionship is needed and silent comfort when silent comfort is needed.

Remember that courtesy is the backbone of good manners. Never jump up onto an Upright's lap until they have made it clear that they are ready to receive you. Although you will, of course, understand everything Uprights say to you, you must never let them know this.

Most important of all, you must never offer them advice. Uprights like cats because we ask no questions and pass no criticisms. They will, perhaps, eventually learn that their friends would like them more if they did the same to them.

Keep your commitments, be just as loyal to those you love when they are not present as you would be when they were. Let your principles run your life and you will not go far wrong. But don't worry too much: remember that if you obey all the rules you will miss rather a lot of the fun.

And remember too that life is under no obligation to give any of us what we expect or think we deserve.

But, most of all, remember this:

I miss you my sweet kitten
Even more than I did fear
I miss your playful ways
Now that you're not here.
Love
Maman

Dear Maman

The Uprights for whom I have taken on responsibility have two smaller Uprights who are both very aggressive and cruel. Today they devised a game which involved stamping on my tail. I didn't enjoy the game very much.

Love

Lemon-Coloured Lion Heart With Long Fine Whiskers

Dear Lemon-Coloured Lion Heart With Long Fine Whiskers

Try to be patient. The smaller Uprights (who are usually referred to as Little Uprights) will, I hope, learn to behave better very quickly. Hopefully the older Uprights will spot their cruelty and teach them to behave with more respect.

Love

Maman

Dear Maman

You and most other cats I know refer to male Uprights as Uprights in Trousers and to female Uprights as the Uprights Who Wear Skirts. But how best should I differentiate between different Uprights? I can always tell Uprights apart very quickly by their smells. All of them have different smells.

Love

Lemon-Coloured Lion Heart With Long Fine Whiskers

Dear Lemon-Coloured Lion Heart With Long Fine Whiskers

When I was a girl we used to refer to the two different types of Uprights as the Uprights in Trousers and the Uprights Who Wear Skirts – those were names which were devised by a cat called Alice who used these names in a diary she published back in the 1980s. But in recent years this nomenclature has become rather out of date. The main problem is that today both types of Upright frequently wear trousers and so it is often difficult to tell the difference between the two sexes. Even Uprights themselves confess that they frequently find it difficult to tell whether an Upright is male or female. (There is no little irony in the fact that I have heard Uprights complain that they find it difficult to tell the difference between male and female cats. How this can be I cannot imagine. I have never, ever in my entire life been confused about the sex of a cat.)

Some cats still use the old-fashioned nomenclature and refer to their Uprights as the Upright in Trousers and the Upright Who Wears a Skirt, but many now prefer to use the simpler, shorter and more precise modern nomenclature, referring to male Uprights as Uprights and female Uprights as Uprightes. As I have already explained human kittens are all known as Little Uprights. It is, of course, perfectly acceptable to add extra bits to the names given to particular Uprights. So, for example, I've always referred to our vet as the Upright With No Hair, though recently this description has lost some value after he started wearing a small patch of fake hair on the top of his head. (Patently false this fake hair is presumably there only to keep the top of his head warm.) But another way to describe Uprights is through their smell. As you have noticed, all Uprights have very characteristic smells and it is perfectly proper to define Uprights by their smells.

Love

Maman

Dear Maman

My Uprights have huge pieces of solid wood in the holes which lead out from the house to the garden. They move these pieces of wood backwards and forwards to suit themselves. When the pieces of wood block off the hole I can't go out (or, if I happen to be outside at the time, come in).

Love

Lemon-Coloured Lion Heart With Long Fine Whiskers

Dear Lemon-Coloured Lion Heart With Long Fine Whiskers

The pieces of wood with which Uprights seal their homes are called 'doors' and, on the whole, only Uprights can open them. (Opening the doors isn't difficult. But the doors are usually too heavy to be moved by a cat.) Most cats who live with Uprights report that the inability to move in and out freely is by far the most consistent and irritating aspect of their lives. No animal – least of all a cat – likes to have their freedom curtailed in any way. It is important, therefore, that cats who enjoy lives both in and out of doors should take early action to make it clear that they are distinctly uncomfortable with this. Sympathetic and thoughtful Uprights will fit a smaller door within the door so that the cat who is looking after them can move in and out of the house whenever it likes.

Love

Maman

Dear Maman

This evening I was trying to climb up onto the chair that my Upright was sitting in when she reached down, picked me up and placed me on her lap. It was warm and as soft as a cushion. There was a lovely smell.

I explored for a few moments and then, as the Upright moved, I slipped and fell. Sitting down seemed so comfortable that I didn't bother to get up. I stayed where I was for twenty minutes. That was, I think, the longest time that I have spent in one place while awake.

I have decided to call my female Upright the Upright Who Smells of Violets. Her husband I will call the Upright Who Smells of Beer.

Love

Lemon-Coloured Lion Heart With Long Fine Whiskers

Dear Lemon-Coloured Lion Heart With Long Fine Whiskers

You have discovered the joy of laps.

I'm so glad you like laps. I'm addicted to them. They are my one supreme vice. Without laps the world would, for me, be a much less interesting, less beautiful and less comfortable place.

I can still remember discovering laps as though it happened yesterday.

I was still a very small kitten – still a little unsteady when I walked but rapidly learning and enjoying the kittenish joys of mischief and fun. I had been jousting with a ball of string which my Uprights had put on the carpet for me to play with and I suddenly felt very, very tired. I had played until I was exhausted and suddenly my energy ran out. It was like someone turning off a light switch. One minute I was furiously kicking at the ball of string with my back legs, the next minute I was flat out on the carpet fast asleep.

I suddenly awoke to find myself being picked up and lifted into the air in a huge, strong, cupped hand. I woke instantly, not because I was frightened (I wasn't because the hand which was holding me was strong and never for one moment did I feel anything but totally secure) but because I was curious and I didn't want to miss anything of what was happening around me.

At the time I had no idea what was happening. All I knew was that I didn't want to miss a second of it.

From the conversation I heard around me it was clear that one of the Uprights had very nearly trodden on me as I lay flat out on the carpet and so one of the others had decided to pick me up and put me somewhere safe.

I listened, for a while, to some discussion about where exactly to put me down. As this went on I stayed aloft, safely held in that firm but gentle hand. Eventually I found myself being lowered, very gently, onto a huge expanse of something much softer and much warmer than I had ever experienced before.

At first I thought that I had been put down on top of a huge cat because I was reminded of nothing quite as much as the time when I had climbed up onto my mother. But as I wandered about, exploring the full extent of the soft surface upon which I had been placed, I quickly discovered that the area belonged not to a cat but to an Upright! I was utterly amazed.

The only parts of Uprights with which I had previously been in contact had been quite hard and unyielding. Nothing had prepared me for the astonishing discovery that in addition to having bony hands, feet and ankles Uprights are also blessed with huge, expanses of warm, softness. Nothing, I discovered, is quite as wonderful as the human lap: it is the first great wonder of the world. For giving us laps Uprights can be forgiven many (if not quite all) of their sins.

The human lap is, I discovered, far, far softer and more yielding than any pillow and just as warm as a hot water bottle (with the added advantage that it stays at just the right temperature indefinitely). I could, if pushed, live in a world without milk, without mice and without butterflies. I could, if I had to, survive in a world without fish, custard and sunshine. But I would not like to have to live in a world without laps. A world without laps would be a dull, uncomfortable place. If I had to choose to spend the rest of my life in one place I would choose a lap; if I had to choose a type of lap I would choose the warm, soft, comfortable lap of a substantial, patient Upright.

My present Upright, is as you will remember, kind, thoughtful and sensitive to my needs. She feeds me well and on time. If she has to go away she never fails to make entirely suitable arrangements. Whenever we move home she makes sure that there is a flap fitted to the kitchen door. Inside the house she always remembers to leave doors open so that I am never shut in one room. She does not skimp on the central heating and she always buys expensive soft furnishings. She chooses soft carpets and bed linen and always fits curtains made of well-secured material which is strong enough to take the weight of a cat. (I know of two cats who have been injured through falls occasioned by weak curtain rails and curtain material of inadequate strength.)

But if there is one thing about her which puts her onto a pedestal and makes her, for me, the perfect Upright it is, without a doubt, her lap.

Sitting on her lap is like sitting on a cloud stuffed with angel dust and love. No cushion could be as comfortable, no sun-soaked window seat quite as perfect. Mice can be too fast and cheese can be too smelly but no lap can be too big or too soft.

Love

Maman

Dear Maman

What do Uprights want from their lives? In my (admittedly modest)

*Sitting on her lap is like sitting on a cloud
stuffed with angel dust and love.*

experience Uprights seem to have a lot of 'stuff' and to rush around a great deal. But what is it all for?

Love

Lemon-Coloured Lion Heart With Long Fine Whiskers

Dear Lemon-Coloured Lion Heart With Long Fine Whiskers

You will find that many Uprights go through their lives without any real purpose. They have many small aims and ambitions of course (probably far more than is good for them) but these are mostly trivial and of a material rather than spiritual nature (they dream of spending two weeks in Tuscany, passing their driving test and buying a widescreen television set with built in woofers and tweeters). But their lives have no real purpose. Funnily enough, many start out with a purpose when they are teenagers. But as they become involved in life's small, daily battles and squabbles, and distracted by the enervating, wearying trivia, they forget their early passions and the purpose they had given themselves. They meander through life rather aimlessly; driven by occasional urges and whimsical temptations; pushed here and there by fashions, fads and fate; rarely if ever remembering the direction in which they had planned to travel or the destination they had dreamt of visiting. Even when they remember, they are invariably too exhausted by the daily trivia, and their own small aims and ambitions, to make the effort to rediscover (let alone regain) their original path. It is surprising how many Uprights (most of whom would not think of leaving home on a journey of a day without a folder full of maps, timetables and tickets) will pursue their arduous journey through life with absolutely no idea where they are heading, or why.

The truth, of course, that Uprights, like cats, can only be effective, and live fulfilling lives, when they know where they want to go. If you don't know where you're heading how can you possibly know when you've got there?

Uprights would get far more out of life if they had a well-defined passion: a mission. Sadly, most are afraid to give themselves a big mission; a desire to change the world and to leave it a better place.

But as a cat you already have such a mission. Your main remaining task is to make sure that you know how you intend to achieve your aim and to fulfil your mission.

Love
Maman

Dear Maman

What should my mission be?

Love
Lemon-Coloured Lion Heart With Long Fine Whiskers

Dear Lemon-Coloured Lion Heart With Long Fine Whiskers

As a cat, living with Uprights, you have a grand and noble mission. Your job is to help teach Uprights how to live their lives and to help them discover some calmness in the constant storm they have made for themselves. You are, in a very real sense, a missionary: a cat put on earth with a blessed vocation.

We should all know what our priorities are and we should run our lives around our priorities, rather than around the trivia. If you watch your Uprights carefully you will see that they will often allow their lives to be ruled by the little things: the big things, the really important things that they care about, get forced into second place by things that really should not and does not matter all that much. They allow themselves to be distracted too easily and they worry endlessly and pointlessly about the uncontrollable. The things which are truly most important should never be at the mercy of things which matter very little. Sadly, the things which Uprights put off are, very often, the things which are really important to them; they get confused between the things which are 'urgent' and the things which are 'important'.

In your life you will find that things which are truly important fall into two categories: those which are urgent (usually unpredictable crises which must necessarily take precedence over everything else) and those which are not urgent and which are easy to put aside.

Planning your life, having ideas, building up relationships, caring for those who are important to you and having fun are all important things. But it is too easy to allow these important things to be pushed aside by things which are really unimportant but which nevertheless seem urgent. If you watch your Uprights carefully you will see that their lives are often organised by and around unimportant things which force their way to the fore and which push more important things to one side.

You must also be true to yourself. And remember that the most important thing a cat puts into any relationship (whether with another cat or an Upright) is not what he or she says or even does, but who they are.

Love

Maman

Dear Maman

What is the difference between right and wrong?

Love

Lemon-Coloured Lion Heart With Long Fine Whiskers

Dear Lemon-Coloured Lion Heart With Long Fine Whiskers

You have to make up your own mind about right and wrong. Set yourself goals and rules that are important to you and then never compromise. Decide what is important to you – integrity, loyalty, honesty, dignity and fairness for example – and make those your values for your life. I believe that it is important for a cat to be trustworthy and reliable, to keep her word and to be prepared to fight for what she believes is right. Be loyal to your family and your friends and your Uprights. Have a real sense of your own identity and a good understanding of your worth. Do your best to defend those who are weaker than you. Always be prepared to learn new things and do your best to improve your existing skills. Learn from your mistakes. Never allow yourself to be bullied or pressured into doing the wrong thing. (And remember that if you aren't doing the right thing you are always doing the wrong thing.) Don't whine when things go wrong, and aim to use up your body and be quite worn out when you die. If you let your conscience take the strain you will find that life is a lot easier.

Know what is important to you. Define your limits and keep to them. In your heart, you will always know the right thing to do. And if you are ever in doubt simply try to treat everyone you meet – whether they be cats or Uprights – with respect and love. Teach by example. Treat everyone as you would like to be treated yourself and you will never go far wrong.

Love

Maman

Dear Maman

I often feel frustrated that although I can understand my Uprights when they talk to me they rarely seem able to understand me when I talk back to them. Oh, they can understand when I want to be fed or want to go out or want a cuddle (and sometimes I pretend to want one when I know *they* need one) but most of the time they don't seem to have the foggiest idea what I'm trying to tell them. I find it frustrating that they have to communicate vocally all the time – it is the only way they can speak to one another. It must be awful for them not to be able to communicate through their minds.

Love

Lemon-Coloured Lion Heart With Long Fine Whiskers

Dear Lemon-Coloured Lion Heart With Long Fine Whiskers

Uprights could communicate telepathically if they put their minds to it. And in due course it will come. But for the time being they are still struggling to understand the power they have and often they go off in the wrong direction. They spend much time searching for answers when often the answers lie not in the outside world but in themselves.

Your inability to speak directly to Uprights is no coincidence; it did not happen by accident. Because you cannot talk directly to your Uprights you will never be tempted to probe, question, interpret, evaluate or advise when you listen. You can just listen. And learning to listen, without being judgemental or feeling the need to offer advice, is something valuable that we cats can teach Uprights. Among Uprights there is often too much talking and not enough listening. They spend much of their lives learning how to talk but very little of it learning how to listen. And yet knowing how to listen – and what to listen for – is crucial. A good listener must try to understand exactly whatever it is the other cat (or Upright) is saying means to them. A good listener must master the art of empathy and must be able to understand what is being said from the speaker's point of view. It doesn't sound easy but it is, in fact, much harder than it sounds. Whatever is important to the other person should be as important to you as they are to you.

Love

Maman

Dear Maman

My new Uprights seem to like playing games.

Today they had four visitors. All six Uprights spent ages with a ball of paper which one of them had tied to a piece of string. I enjoyed the game (it made them very happy when I joined in) but I am afraid I eventually tired before they did. I clambered onto the lap of a large Upright Who Smelt of Lavender and went straight to sleep.

Now I feel quite bad about this.

Do you think they will be offended?

Love

Lemon-Coloured Lion Heart With Long Fine Whiskers

Dear Lemon-Coloured Lion Heart With Long Fine Whiskers

Don't worry in the slightest about falling asleep in the middle of a game with your Uprights. It is true that Uprights think it rude if another of their species falls asleep on a social occasion but they find it endearing if a cat falls asleep. And they find it *very* endearing if a kitten falls asleep. Indeed, most Uprights find everything a kitten

Uprights think it rude if another of their species falls asleep at a social occasion, but they find it endearing if a cat falls asleep.

does endearing so you really don't have to worry about making social gaffes.

Love
Maman

Dear Maman

There is a cat in my neighbourhood who is huge. He struts around as though he owns everyone and everything. He's big, he's strong, he's fast and he's bright. I feel very inferior to him. I don't like him or admire him because he has a reputation as quite a bully. But I am frightened of him. Have you ever felt like this? How should I deal with the problem?

Love
Lemon-Coloured Lion Heart With Long Fine Whiskers

Dear Lemon-Coloured Lion Heart With Long Fine Whiskers

When I was quite a young cat I lived for a while in a house in a town near the sea. There were quite a few cats in our neighbourhood and we all had one thing in common: we were all absolutely terrified of a huge, old tomcat called Hercules.

Hercules was absolutely enormous and he was a ferocious fellow; very bad tempered and always aggressive. No one got on with him at all. He was a bully and for months and months I was terrified of him. I used to wake up at night shivering with fear after imagining that he had chased me into the nearby park. Things got so bad that I would never wander far from the house. I liked to stay close to home so that I could make a run for my catflap if I spotted Hercules. He was tough but he wasn't tough enough to follow a cat through her own cat flap.

And then something happened that changed everything.

I was out walking in the garden one morning, communing with nature as your grand-mère always used to say, when it started to rain. I decided that rather than race back to my own house I would just slip into next door's garage. The Upright who lived there always left the doors open when he took his car out in the morning and

We were all absolutely terrified
of a huge, old tomcat called Hercules.

didn't close them until he put his car back in at night. In those days Uprights often left doors open. Today no one would leave a garage door open unless they wanted to get rid of everything in the garage. Upright thieves will steal anything – even an oil stain – these days.

Anyway, this was then and the doors were open. There was a large roll of old carpet in the garage, stored with a ladder and some lengths of drain pipe on two storage racks firmly fastened to the wall. I had found that it was possible to get up onto the carpet by taking three, fairly daring, leaps from the floor to a window sill, from the window sill to the top of a cupboard at the back of the garage and from the top of the cupboard to the roll of carpet. It was not only as comfortable a spot as I had ever found but from the top of the carpet there was a terrific view over the whole of the garage and the area of the drive just in front of it.

I curled up on the carpet and settled down to enjoy the sight and sound of the rain. I have found few things in life which give me greater pleasure than being inside, in the dry and warm, when outside it is raining and blowing and generally miserable. Being just a few inches away from the rain, in an open garage, summerhouse or shed, does, for some reason which I have never understood, make the whole experience even more enjoyable.

I had only been established on my perch for a few minutes when, to my absolute horror, Hercules strolled into the garage, shook himself and tucked himself up behind a bicycle. As you can imagine I was terrified. I had no idea how long Hercules would stay there but I suspected it might be until it stopped raining. And what if it didn't stop raining until the evening? I would be trapped in the garage. What if Hercules looked up, decided to explore a little, and found me? What if he simply smelt me? Most cats know when there is another feline around and I strongly suspected that Hercules would be no exception to this rule.

But it quickly became apparent that Hercules was unaware of my presence and was far more interested in something else: a vole which had also decided to take shelter from the rain.

Hercules had a grand reputation as a hunter and I was curious to see how he would catch the vole – for catch it I was sure he would. I watched carefully, hardly daring to breathe, as he crept out from behind the bicycle and slowly worked his way into a position from which he could pounce. It didn't look as though the vole was aware of his presence at all.

But then something extraordinary happened.

Just as Hercules made his move the vole turned, leapt up and bit him.

Hercules, bleeding, astonished and clearly stunned retreated a couple of feet. The vole, instead of taking advantage of the moment and running away, launched himself at Hercules and grabbed hold of the bully's nose with his teeth. He held on for what seemed like a lifetime but was, I suppose, no more than half a minute at the most. Hercules, squealed and screeched and tried in vain to get the vole off his nose. He ran around the garage in great distress.

Eventually, just as suddenly as it had started, the drama was over. The vole let go of Hercules's nose and strolled calmly out of the garage. Hercules, in a state of shock, just stood where he was, blood dripping from his nose, and stared as the vole disappeared from view.

Just then the carpet upon which I was sitting moved a fraction of an inch and a tiny flurry of dust drifted down to the floor. Hercules looked up and saw me immediately. I had no time at all to move or to hide.

I could tell straight away that Hercules knew that I had seen everything. I think he contemplated leaping up onto the shelf, the cupboard and the carpet so that he could attack me but he abandoned the idea almost as soon as he had it; his heart wasn't in it. He slunk out of the garage with his tail, quite literally between his legs. He had come into the garage a bully, but he left it a coward.

The next day he came looking for me. He found me in next door's garden, sitting by their goldfish pond, sunbathing.

'Have you told anyone?' he asked me.

I did think about lying. I wondered if he might attack me and try to kill me to keep me silent if I confessed that I hadn't told anyone what I'd seen. But I told him the truth. 'No,' I assured him.

For the first time since I had known Hercules I wasn't frightened of him. I actually felt sorry for him. I could see he felt terrible.

'Thank you,' he said.

I didn't say anything.

'I wasn't expecting the vole to attack,' he told me, 'not at that precise moment.'

I nodded but didn't say anything.

'I feel very embarrassed,' he said.

'I expect so,' I agreed.

'I've been thinking of moving away,' he said. 'But word travels fast.'

'I won't say anything,' I told him. 'Not if you stop bullying.'

'I don't bully!' he said.

I looked at him but didn't say or even think anything.

'OK,' he said. His thoughts were hardly audible.

And then he left. Three years later he died defending a tortoiseshell and her two kittens from an attack led by two Doberman dogs. From the day the vole bit him he never bullied anyone again.

And from that day on something happened to me too. I never again felt inferior to anyone. I never again felt frightened. And because I didn't feel inferior and never felt frightened of another cat I never got bullied again.

Just remember Lemon-Coloured Lion Heart With Long Fine Whiskers: another cat may be faster than you, stronger than you or even prettier than you (though I think that is unlikely) but no cat will ever be *better* than you. Every cat has his or her weakness. Even the toughest cat is frightened of something. I once knew a ginger tom who was a veteran of scores of dog fights but who was terrified of spiders. Every bully has the skeleton of a vole in a cupboard somewhere. If you let a bully know that you know that behind the bluster and the bravado there is just as much fear as there is in a kitten then the bully will stop bullying. A bully's greatest fear is that you will call his bluff and let him know that he cannot frighten you.

Love

Maman

Dear Maman

My Uprights have had to go away for a weekend and have left me to look after a friend of theirs. She is very well-meaning but rather nervous and worries a good deal. I took to her just as soon as we met. She has soft hands and a warm lap and is clearly a very loving and caring person. She has a small allotment where she grows beautiful pink roses.

As I sat dozing on her lap I could not help noticing that she was slowly becoming increasingly nervous and agitated. Eventually, her agitation became so intense that she could no longer sit still. She gently lifted me off her lap, stood up and walked out of the room. A few moments later I heard her talking on the telephone in the hallway.

I had no idea that her agitation had anything to do with me and so it would be an understatement to say that I was surprised when an Upright Who Smells of Disinfectant arrived. I don't think I have been so shocked since the day when Sleeping Beige Silken Fur scratched the nose of a Doberman and sent him snivelling back behind his Upright with his tail between his legs. I was curled up on the chair on which the Upright had been sitting, though the chair's cushion was, of course, nowhere near as comfortable as the Upright's lap.

'I'm very worried,' my temporary Upright Who Smells of Pink Roses whispered to the Upright Who Smells of Disinfectant. 'She's not doing it now, but when she was on my lap she was making a very funny noise. It sounded as though she's got something stuck in her throat.'

'See if you can get the cat to make the same sound again,' suggested the Upright Who Smells of Disinfectant. 'Sit down and put her on your lap.'

And so the Upright Who Smells of Pink Roses carefully lifted me up into the air, sat down and then gently replaced me on her lap. Within a few minutes I had relaxed and was once again feeling comfortable, calm and relaxed.

'There it is!' said the Upright Who Smells of Pink Roses suddenly. 'She's doing it again.'

'She's purring,' explained the Upright Who Smells of Disinfectant.

'Purring?' said the Upright Who Smells of Pink Roses.

'It's a noise cats make,' said the Upright Who Smells of Disinfectant. 'Usually when they're happy.'

'So it isn't anything to worry about?' said the Upright Who Smells of Pink Roses, sounding extremely relieved.

'It definitely isn't anything to worry about,' said the Upright Who Smells of Disinfectant with a big smile in his voice.

'Oh, that's a relief,' said the Upright Who Smells of Pink Roses, sounding reassured. 'I'm looking after her for friends,' she explained. 'I'm terrified that something might happen to her while they're away.' She started to lift me up. 'I'll see you out,' she said to the Upright Who Smells of Disinfectant.

'Don't you worry. And don't move an inch,' said the Upright Who Smells of Disinfectant, holding out a hand to indicate that my temporary Upright should stay where she was. 'I'll see myself out and slam the door behind me.' There was a pause. 'And, by the way,' he added, 'she's a he.'

I have to confess that I felt very silly when the Upright Who Smells of Disinfectant had gone. I even wondered whether there was something wrong with my purring. I even tried to stop purring for a while but Upright Who Smells of Pink Roses had such a very comfortable lap that I'm afraid my resolve did not last for long.

Love

Lemon-Coloured Lion Heart With Long Fine Whiskers

Dear Lemon-Coloured Lion Heart With Long Fine Whiskers

There was no need at all for you to feel silly. Some Uprights really don't know very much about us at all, but you must always remember that it is our task to teach Uprights about cats and while it is our main responsibility to try to teach Uprights some of our values, we must also teach them about us as beings.

The Upright's anxiety about your purring was exacerbated by the fact that when she met you she knew almost nothing at all about cats. You and I know that you were there to teach her but naturally, like so many Uprights who know little about cats, she didn't understand this. Instead, obviously a kindly Upright, she was clearly overwhelmed by what she perceived as her responsibility both to you and to your usual Uprights.

Purr away, my sweet darling. You have a lovely purr. Be proud to purr whenever the fancy takes you.

Incidentally, your Upright Who Smells of Pink Roses sounds lovely and caring. What a pity you cannot stay with her.

Love

Maman

Dear Maman

How I wish I could stay with the Upright Who Smells of Pink Roses. I know I could be very happy with her – and I could make her happy too. But she has told friends that although she loves having me with her and would like to keep me, she cannot because I belong to other Uprights.

The Little Uprights have stopped stamping on my tail. They now have a new game which involves chasing me, catching me and then painting bizarrely coloured stripes onto my fur. It takes a considerable amount of time for me to lick off these painted stripes. And I usually end up swallowing so much paint that I am sick afterwards.

Love

Lemon-Coloured Lion Heart With Long Fine Whiskers

Dear Lemon-Coloured Lion Heart With Long Fine Whiskers

You have my sympathy. The only comfort I can offer you is that Little Uprights usually get tired of such games. Meanwhile, I encourage you to be patient.

Love

Maman

The fact is that cats are never overweight.
Some are big boned (left)
and some have hormone problems (centre)
and some have water retention problems (right).

Dear Maman

I'm getting a little podgy. Do you think this is anything to worry about? My friend Shimmering Fur Chantelle says that I should try the new 'green food diet' which, she claims, is all the rage in New York. She says that if I only eat food which is green I will be able to lose up to two ounces a week.

Love
Lemon-Coloured Lion Heart With Long Fine Whiskers

Dear Lemon-Coloured Lion Heart With Long Fine Whiskers

I don't think there is a species on earth which is quite so conscious of appearance as cats. Uprights think they worry about how they look but in my experience there isn't an Upright alive who comes anywhere near to a cat when it comes to worrying about their appearance. Some folk would call it vanity. I prefer to think of it as taking a natural and entirely justified pride in one's appearance.

The fact is that cats are never overweight. Some are big-boned, some have hormone problems and some have water retention problems. But, despite this cats are always trying out new diets. One spring just a few years ago the Catkins Diet was all the rage. Cats everywhere were eating catkins and claiming that as a result they were losing weight. I thought it was very silly and quite possibly dangerous and so it eventually proved to be. Tragically, the cat who had started the Catkins Diet was quite young and grossly overweight when he died.

The truth is that dieting is usually unnecessary and quite unsuitable for cats. There are only two rules which fat cats must always remember. The first is that they should never be ashamed or embarrassed by their size. Plump cats who remain confident and assured will always look good. The second (and most overweight cats know this instinctively) rule is to arrange themselves in a slim way.

Love
Maman

A cat should always respond when their Upright calls –
unless they have something better to do, of course.

Dear Maman

Should I always run to them when my Uprights call for me? I always hear them, of course, but sometimes they call at very inconvenient times. I confess that once or twice I have pretended not to have heard them. Is this forgivable?

Love
Lemon-Coloured Lion Heart With Long Fine Whiskers

Dear Lemon-Coloured Lion Heart With Long Fine Whiskers

As Glacier Blue Princess, a wonderfully wise Siamese cat who lived in the 1960s once said: 'A cat should always respond when their Upright calls – unless they have something better to do, of course.'

Love
Maman

Dear Maman

I woke up a few moments ago feeling lonely and sad. I miss you so much. I find it very difficult to accept that I will never see you again. It is good to be able to 'talk' to you whenever I want but I don't ever know where you are and I miss being able to touch you and cuddle into your fur. This probably sounds strange but if I knew how to find you, and I knew I could find you whenever I wanted to, I would, I think, be much better able to cope without seeing you...

Love
Lemon-Coloured Lion Heart With Long Fine Whiskers

Dear Lemon-Coloured Lion Heart With Long Fine Whiskers

I understand your feelings. But you could find me very easily if you really needed to. (And knowing that should make the absence easier to bear.) Uprights are always astonished and puzzled about how we do it but cats can always find their way back home. All you have to do is concentrate hard and head towards the source of a felipathic transmission. The closer you get the stronger the signal will become. If, for any reason, you cannot communicate with me all you have to do is link up with another cat in the neighbourhood. There is, for example, Winged Tortoiseshell who lives two doors down to our left or Dancing Feather who lives across the road. In the absence of live felipathic guidance all you have to do is call up one of our old felipathic messages and use that as a directional aid. Stored messages aren't as powerful as live ones but they work perfectly well.

Love

Maman

P.S. You are still practising your sounds, aren't you? I don't like to nag but it is important that you practise your sounds regularly. To Uprights nothing expresses contentment more surely than a purr and nothing expresses need or demand more than a plaintive miaow. You should practise both these sounds at least an hour a day. Try to find a quiet spot where you won't be overheard or you will find that your practice sessions will be constantly interrupted with cuddles and saucers of milk. I know all this practising can seem tiresome but just try to remember that a cat who can purr well and miaow with feeling will never go hungry or short of servants.

Dear Maman

Tell me about the first time you caught a mouse, Maman.

Love

Lemon-Coloured Lion Heart With Long Fine Whiskers

Dear Lemon-Coloured Lion Heart With Long Fine Whiskers

I've told you about that a thousand times!

Love

Maman

Dear Maman

I know. But I love hearing about it. Please tell me the story again.

Love

Lemon-Coloured Lion Heart With Long Fine Whiskers

Dear Lemon-Coloured Lion Heart With Long Fine Whiskers

All right. (From her voice it is clear that she is smiling.) Are you lying comfortably?

Love

Maman

Dear Maman

I am, Maman.

Love

Lemon-Coloured Lion Heart With Long Fine Whiskers

Dear Lemon-Coloured Lion Heart With Long Fine Whiskers

It happened a long, long time ago. I was just a few weeks older than you are now and I was very, very innocent and inexperienced. I had for as long as I could remember been worrying about how and when I was going to catch my first mouse. I knew it had to happen eventually, of course. And I knew that when the time came I would know instinctively what to do. But none of that stopped me worrying. My best friend, a pretty, long-haired blue Persian called Dancing Light In Bluebell Woods, was two weeks younger than me and she'd already caught her first mouse. She never stopped talking about it and although I wanted to be happy for her, and always tried my best to look pleased when she told her story, I sometimes silently wished she wouldn't go on about it quite so much. I remember suffering terrible guilt for feeling that way. Uprights often say that cats never suffer from guilt but they don't know the half of it. Young kittens often feel guilty.

It wasn't just Dancing Light In Bluebell Woods who had already caught her first mouse. It sometimes seemed as though every kitten I knew had already caught at least one mouse. A kitten whom I knew vaguely, a very confident jet black short hair called Ebony the Hunter, who was a week younger than me, claimed that he had caught four mice and eaten every single one of them. I remember sitting in the gloaming one evening listening to him tell how he'd been terribly ill after his first mouse. 'After the third, you acquire a taste for them,' he confided, in an annoyingly cocky way. I remember feeling awful after that. Now I not only had to worry about catching my first mouse but I also had to worry about how I would feel after I had eaten it. It was Ebony the Hunter whose confidence and self-assurance did most to make me feel inadequate. His bragging (which I didn't think of as bragging at the time) made me feel like a failure before I'd even started.

For a while after that I kept away from other cats. Whenever I saw Ebony the Hunter I would hide and I even went out of my way to avoid Dancing Light In Bluebell Woods who had for weeks been my very best and dearest friend. I deliberately ignored the messages they, and others, sent me. I became quite introspective, almost depressed I suppose. I stayed indoors and pretended I had a sore paw when the Uprights wondered why I no longer went out into the garden. They were so worried about me that one evening they even took me to the Upright Who Smells of Disinfectant. The Upright Who Smells of Disinfectant, a kindly old Upright who always reeked extra strongly of disinfectant so that the Uprights wouldn't smell the whisky on his breath, said he thought I'd bruised my paw jumping down from too great a height. I was certain he knew there was nothing wrong with me and I suspected even then that he knew what was really the matter. He understood cats. The modern Uprights Who Smell of Disinfectant, all brisk manners, white coats and steroid injections, may know how to read laboratory results but they aren't a patch on the old ones when it comes to really understanding how a cat feels.

My self-imposed isolation went on, I suppose, for about a fortnight. And then I woke up one morning and realised that I just couldn't go on this way. I gave myself a firm ticking off and made myself go out into the garden and do some serious hunting.

I headed for the area the Uprights rather grandly described as their orchard. In reality it was just a few scruffy apple trees behind the garden shed. Most of the trees were dead or dying and looking back I doubt if they'd produced more than a basketful of apples between them for some years. There were quite a few dead branches on the ground and what grass there was between the trees was long and straggly. Actually, there wasn't much grass at all; much of it had been pushed aside by huge, tough thistles which seemed to stretch high into the sky like miniature trees, and impenetrable forests of stinging nettles. In the area immediately behind the garden shed the Uprights kept all sorts of unwanted stuff: broken earthenware plant pots, piled high and stored for some possible, undefined, future use; rolls of netting, now rusting and overgrown with bindweed; a rusting wheelbarrow, with a wheel missing and a large, jagged hole in one side; a coil of green hose pipe; two rusting watering cans; a pail with no handle; four sheets of corrugated iron and a pile of rotting wooden fence posts.

It was there, I knew, that huge families of mice resided. Ebony the Hunter used to call it 'Mouse City' and said that no mouser worth his or her salt would go hunting there because it was like shooting fish in a barrel. I didn't understand why anyone would want to shoot fish in a barrel (an activity which, however much harm it did to the fish, seemed destined to do almost as much harm to the barrel) or what shooting fish in a barrel had to do with catching mice behind the garden shed but that's what Ebony the Hunter said and since he had caught (and eaten) not one but four mice neither I nor any of the others had the courage to question his wisdom.

Actually, it took no little courage for me to go there at all because, as I remembered only too well, Ebony the Hunter frequently used to tell us horror stories about the size of the rats which, he claimed, shared the potting shed with the mice. He said that he had personally seen rats there bigger than Black Night with Grey Chest (the biggest tomcat any of us had ever seen) and that he had it on very good authority (naturally, he didn't say on whose authority) that the pack of rats which lived there used to go out on dark nights and catch Uprights which they would then drag back into the nettles and eat while the blood was still pumping out of them. When questioned he said that when they had eaten all the flesh they buried the bones so that no one would ever know what they'd done. I knew this was nonsense, of course, but even lying on a comfortable cushion on a chair in the living room, I would sometimes awaken shaking with fear as images of huge, Upright-eating rats stormed my dreams and turned them into nightmares. Crouching there in the long grass, alone and anxious, I felt sure that the sound of my beating heart must surely waken the entire neighbourhood. The whole area was crawling with beetles, spiders, aphids and crickets and humming with the sound of wasps and bees buzzing about their business.

I had been crouching on the pile of rotting fence posts for I suppose, five minutes or so (it seemed more like five hours, of course) when I became aware that there was something large and dark crawling through the grass, below me and a little distance to my right. I couldn't see who or what it was. I froze for a moment. I remember thinking that the monster – whoever or whatever it was – would need to be deaf not to have heard my beating heart. Boom, boom, boom, boom, my heart seemed to go. Canon fire would have made less noise and been less obvious. Suddenly, the monster moved. It moved apparently without any care for who knew it was there. The grass around it shook as though in an earthquake.

Terrified, and acting entirely out of instinct and an acute sense of self-preservation, I leapt down from the rotting fence posts into the grass, hoping that if I was fast enough I might be able to escape from the monster. The fact that the unseen creature was clearly making no attempt to hide its presence only heightened my anxiety. Most animals, other than perhaps lions, elephants and rhinos, move circumspectly, careful not to advertise their presence to would-be predators.

I landed right on top of two long-tailed field mice which had, quite unknown to me, been quietly gorging themselves in the shadow of the pile of wood. My fear of the unseen monster temporarily evaporated and I looked down at the two mice in astonishment. They looked back at me. They were both winded and stunned. For a moment I didn't quite know what to do. Then, quite without provocation, one of the mice regained its composure, leapt at me and bit me on the nose. Astonished and stinging I instinctively lashed out with my right front paw and a moment later mouse lay on the ground before me. My first kill. The second mouse looked up at me and crouched as though ready to leap. This time I was ready

*I landed right on top of two long-tailed field mice which had,
quite unbeknown to me, been quietly gorging themselves
in the shadow of the pile of wood.*

and a second or two later my second kill lay before me.

'You stole my mice!' protested a voice I knew. I turned my head to the left. Ebony the Hunter was staring at the two mice which now lay dead in front of me.

'You stole them!' he said, clearly furious.

'Where were you?' I asked.

'Just over there. I've been stalking those two mice for ages,' said Ebony the Hunter. I suddenly realised that Ebony the Hunter had been the monster which had so alarmed me.

'I didn't see you,' I told him.

'That's because I was stalking,' said Ebony the Hunter. 'I was being quiet.'

I remembered the noise the 'monster' had made, crashing through the grass.

Unexpectedly, Ebony the Hunter began to cry. 'I was going to catch one of those,' he said, nodding in the direction of the two mice. 'One of them would have been mine.'

'I'm sorry,' I said. 'If I'd seen you there I wouldn't have made a move.' It didn't seem necessary to admit that I had literally landed on the two mice by accident.

Ebony the Hunter made a rather pathetic, whimpering sound.

'Why are you so upset?' I asked him. 'You've already caught four mice. These were my first! And I'm a week older than you are.'

Ebony the Hunter didn't say anything. Tears rolled down his cheek and his head dropped disconsolately. 'I haven't caught any mice,' he said.

I looked at him, disbelievingly. 'Say that again?'

'I haven't caught any mice.'

'If you'd caught one of these it would have been your first?'

'Yes.'

'Your very first?'

'Yes.'

I stared at him, then at the two mice.

'You said you'd caught four!'

'I exaggerated a bit.'

'And eaten them all!'

'I said that in case anyone said they hadn't seen the bodies.'

'You ate the evidence because there wasn't any?'

'Yes.'

I looked at him and felt sorry for him.

'Why don't we say we caught one each?' I suggested.

He looked up and blinked. 'You'd do that? You'd let me have one of your mice?'

I nodded. 'I don't think I can carry two anyway,' I said.

We picked up a mouse each and headed back into the garden. During the next hour or two we showed our mice to everyone we could find.

Ebony the Hunter and I became firm friends after that. We often went hunting and three days later we caught our second mice together. Today, Ebony the Hunter is a professional mouser on a farm in the Lake District but we still 'talk' several times a week.

Love

Maman

Dear Maman

I caught my first mouse today. I am feeling very proud of myself.

Love

Lemon-Coloured Lion Heart With Long Fine Whiskers

Dear Lemon-Coloured Lion Heart With Long Fine Whiskers

You should be proud. I am very proud of you too.

Love

Maman

Dear Maman

Are all Uprights incapable of learning how to hunt? It seems curious (and sad) that such large creatures should be unable to catch mice.

Love

Lemon-Coloured Lion Heart With Long Fine Whiskers

Dear Lemon-Coloured Lion Heart With Long Fine Whiskers

No. It is sometimes possible to teach Uprights the rudiments of hunting. But I've never known an Upright become more than vaguely competent at catching mice. One of the main problems is the fact (rather surprising I know) that most Uprights are actually frightened of mice. There is no logic to this because Uprights are much bigger than mice. But logic is not a quality normally associated with Uprights.

Love

Maman

Dear Maman

Today, I am afraid I lost my temper with the Little Uprights. They have both been given water pistols as presents and, naturally, they decided that I should be their first and only target. After being soaked several times I chased them both. I hissed at them both until they cried, and then scratched one on the arm and one on the upper leg. I feel really ashamed.

Love

Lemon-Coloured Lion Heart With Long Fine Whiskers

Dear Lemon-Coloured Lion Heart With Long Fine Whiskers

I think you did very well to last as long as you did. Please don't feel ashamed.

Love

Maman

Dear Maman

My shame is complete. My Uprights are sending me to another home. They say they are doing this because I am not suitable for a house where there are Little Uprights. I was in the room when the Little Uprights showed their scratches to their parents. They complained that they had been sitting reading and that I had suddenly attacked them, and scratched them, without any provocation. The Uprights believed the Little Uprights completely.

I had to endure a long speech from the Upright Who Smells of Violets. She told me that they were very disappointed with me; she said that they had welcomed me into their family and treated me kindly and that she and her husband felt that I had let them down.

Love
Lemon-Coloured Lion Heart With Long Fine Whiskers

Dear Lemon-Coloured Lion Heart With Long Fine Whiskers

I love you and always will.

Love
Maman

Dear Maman

My new Uprights are quite nice. But they already have a dog who does not seem particularly pleased to see me. I have christened my new Uprights the Upright Who Smells of Soap and the Upright Who Smells of Oil.

Love
Lemon-Coloured Lion Heart With Long Fine Whiskers

Dear Lemon-Coloured Lion Heart With Long Fine Whiskers

Be patient. It can take time to settle into a household. Try to remember that the dog who is already in residence may rather resent your arrival – and be frightened that you might take too much of the attention. Try to make it clear that you recognise your position.

Love
Maman

Dear Maman

The Uprights seem to talk a great deal about the future. They are always worrying about something that might happen in the future. They spend much of their lives worrying about tomorrow, and trying to make sure that there aren't any problems, but when tomorrow comes they spend it worrying about tomorrow and the problems it might bring.

Love

Lemon-Coloured Lion Heart With Long Fine Whiskers

Dear Lemon-Coloured Lion Heart With Long Fine Whiskers

Your job here on earth is to try to teach Uprights new values and to try to help them to understand how to manage their lives so that they find more peace and contentment and suffer less from anxiety. Your immediate aim is to teach your Uprights that if they look after the minutes and the hours then the days and weeks and months and years will all look after themselves.

Love

Maman

Dear Maman

Training Uprights sounds like very hard work.

Love

Lemon-Coloured Lion Heart With Long Fine Whiskers

Dear Lemon-Coloured Lion Heart With Long Fine Whiskers

It's not as difficult as you probably imagine. Always reward good behaviour or kindness. Intangibles make by far the best rewards for Uprights. Plenty of purring and some enthusiastic treadling are invariably far better received than fresh mice on the paw or even a freshly and neatly disembowelled rabbit.

Love

Maman

Dear Maman

When the Uprights have prepared food for themselves is it all right for a cat to help himself? The other night the Upright Who Smells of Soap prepared a chicken for their evening meal. The chicken smelt wonderful and so while the Uprights were in the dining room

I jumped onto the kitchen table and helped myself to a little of the chicken that was left. When the Upright Who Smells of Soap came into the kitchen with the empty plates she shouted at me and seemed very upset.

enjoying their meal I jumped up onto the kitchen table and helped myself to a little of the chicken that was left. When the Upright Who Smells of Soap came into the kitchen with the empty plates she shouted at me and seemed very upset.

Love

Lemon-Coloured Lion Heart With Long Fine Whiskers

Dear Lemon-Coloured Lion Heart With Long Fine Whiskers

Generally speaking it is best to wait to be asked before tasting food Uprights have prepared for themselves. There are three reasons for this. First, Uprights have remarkably undeveloped taste buds and some of the food they eat is hideously unpleasant. Wise Uprights recognise this and will not offer you food unless they think you might like it. Second, if you eat food a few minutes after an Upright has tasted it you can be fairly sure it is not going to poison you. Uprights' stomachs tend to be extraordinarily sensitive. (I have met Uprights who could not face the prospect of eating a freshly killed field mouse.) Finally, Uprights are rather proprietorial about their food. They are likely to show displeasure (even distress) if you eat food they have prepared for themselves before they have got round to eating it.

Love

Maman

Dear Maman

Is it a bad thing for a cat to have a good time? I have two friends called Great White Paws and Nutmeg Fluffy Fur. This afternoon Nutmeg Fluffy Fur was telling us about the way she spends her days. She wakes at eight and has a large breakfast. She then sleeps until one when she has a large lunch. She then has a nap until four when she pops outside to potter around the garden for half an hour. She then goes back indoors for another nap before dinner at six. After six she takes a nap on a lap until bedtime at ten thirty. Great White Paws was quite scornful and told Nutmeg Fluffy Fur that he thought she was terribly self-indulgent. Nutmeg Fluffy Fur said she didn't see what was wrong with her lifestyle. She said she thought she was setting Uprights an excellent example. 'If more Uprights lived the way I do there would be no wars, no fights, no conflict, no violence and no disagreements,' she insisted.

Love

Lemon-Coloured Lion Heart With Long Fine Whiskers

Dear Lemon-Coloured Lion Heart With Long Fine Whiskers

Your Great Aunt Cinnamon Flecks and Noble Spirit (who was, I admit, known to everyone as Mathilda) believed that self-indulgence was a virtue. She argued that if there was ever any such thing as an ascetic cat it would be the most miserable creature on the planet. 'A miserable cat is of no use to anyone,' she said. 'Our job is to train Uprights and to help educate them. What Uprights would want to spend time with a cat who was constantly moaning and whining? The cat who indulges herself, and gives in to all her desires, will always be happy, better able equipped to spread purrs and contentment among those around her, and far more skilled at training Uprights.' Your Great Aunt Mathilda followed her own philosophy very closely. She once took me on one side and gave me what she said was her very best advice. 'My kitten,' she said, eyes closed in delighted anticipation as she sniffed a plate of steamed plaice which her Upright had prepared for her, 'always remember that too much of a good thing is simply wonderful.'

Love

Maman

Dear Maman

I like chasing my tail. Do you know if a cat has ever caught its tail? My friend Great White Paws says that it's silly and pointless for a cat to chase its own tail. He says I should be ashamed and embarrassed and that I should join him and all the other local cats in sensible pastimes such as taunting dogs and eating butterflies.

Love

Lemon-Coloured Lion Heart With Long Fine Whiskers

Dear Lemon-Coloured Lion Heart With Long Fine Whiskers

Only when you know why you do things will you know whether the things you are doing are really worth doing. If you do something because it's fun and you enjoy doing it, then that's a good reason for doing it. If you do it because it's good exercise, and excellent hunting practice, then that's a good reason for doing it too.

On the other hand, if you do something solely because other cats want you to do it, then that isn't a good reason. If you do something because other cats do it, that isn't a good reason.

You should only ever be embarrassed or ashamed if you do things solely because others tell you that you should.

Love

Maman

Dear Maman

Today I met a black and white short hair who lives nearby. His Uprights call him Toby but his real name is Plump, Sleepy Cat Who Moves Like A Proud Eagle. He is nearly a year old and much bigger than I am. He wants me to go into a nearby park with him. He says there is a lake in the park and that there are bound to be fish in the lake. He says we can catch some of the fish and have a nice meal out.

I am tempted to go with him but, although I don't know why, I do have reservations.

Plump, Sleepy Cat Who Moves Like A Proud Eagle says I am unwilling to because I am frightened. But I don't know what I'm frightened of.

Love

Lemon-Coloured Lion Heart With Long Fine Whiskers

Dear Lemon-Coloured Lion Heart With Long Fine Whiskers

Fear is nothing to be ashamed of. A lot of cats would live longer, happier lives if they took more notice of their fears and listened to their instincts. Don't let yourself be bullied or shamed into doing something you don't want to do. Remember: if you make sure you always do the right thing you will be unlikely ever to do the wrong thing.

Love

Maman

Dear Maman

I heard today that Plump, Sleepy Cat Who Moves Like A Proud Eagle (the cat who wanted me to go to fishing in the park with him) died yesterday. He went to the park, climbed along a low branch overhanging the lake and fell into the water when the branch broke. He couldn't swim. Now I am full of guilt. Maybe, if I had gone with him I might have been able to save him.

Love

Lemon-Coloured Lion Heart With Long Fine Whiskers

Dear Lemon-Coloured Lion Heart With Long Fine Whiskers

Can you swim?

Love

Maman

Dear Maman

No.

Love

Lemon-Coloured Lion Heart With Long Fine Whiskers

Dear Lemon-Coloured Lion Heart With Long Fine Whiskers

If you had tried to save Plump, Sleepy Cat Who Moves Like A Proud Eagle you would have almost certainly drowned too. Then the world would have had two less cats – instead of one less cat. And that would have been double the catastrophe. Your instincts were right and saved you and I am glad you listened to them. You should always listen to your instincts.

Love

Maman

Dear Maman

My Uprights had visitors last weekend. The visitors were very dull indeed. I was bored.
      Love
      Lemon-Coloured Lion Heart With Long Fine Whiskers

Dear Lemon-Coloured Lion Heart With Long Fine Whiskers

Please don't let me hear you say that again. You should never be bored. There is no such thing as an uninteresting Upright; there are only uninterested cats. Watch and listen and you will always find something to learn from every Upright you meet. And you should never be bored when you are away from Uprights either. Life is full of exciting and wonderful things. In daytime try to count the different shades of green in the garden. At night look up at the sky and count the stars. Lie in the garden and listen to the sounds you never normally hear. Watch the sunrise from a branch above a dewy lawn and then, later the same day, watch the sunset from the same spot. Remember how excited you were when you were a tiny kitten, feeling life all around you, awaking every morning full of a new sense of excitement; touching life with every nerve in your body, smelling it, seeing it, running with it and through it and feeling it all around you and in everything you did.
      Love
      Maman

Dear Maman

There is a new dog living next door. He is small but noisy. I have tried to make friends with him but he spurns all my advances. He really doesn't seem to like me. Every day, when he sees me, he barks and barks and barks. I think he would kill me if he could. Do you think I should persevere in trying to be nice to him?
      Love
      Lemon-Coloured Lion Heart With Long Fine Whiskers

Dear Lemon-Coloured Lion Heart With Long Fine Whiskers

Don't waste valuable time and effort loving your enemies. They won't love you back; your efforts will be wasted, you will feel frustrated and disappointed and your enemies will think you are weak and will treat you with even less respect. Instead, of wasting love on your enemies give the extra love to your friends. They will thank you and love you back.

Love

Maman

Dear Maman

Sometimes I don't think I will ever understand Uprights. Today, we had visitors – two large ones and three small ones. The small ones were noisy and rather frightening so I kept well away from them. But one of the Upright visitors seemed rather friendly. She was kind, gentle and, as my friend Great White Paws would put it, comfortably upholstered. When she, together with the other three adult Uprights sat down, I thought I'd try out her lap. Sometimes a new lap can be very refreshing. My Uprights expressed considerable surprise at this and made numerous comments to their guest, pointing out to her that she should regard herself as being exceptionally honoured. The lap she provided was so very comfortable that I stayed there for quite a while – not because I thought I ought to or because I wanted to make the visitors feel at home but simply because the lap was exceedingly comfortable. In the end I actually fell asleep. I woke to find myself being gently lifted and placed down on the carpet by the owner of the lap which I had occupied. The visiting Uprights then headed for their automobile. After hugging and kissing and shaking paws and crying, as it is now clear to me our Uprights do to mark the slightest of partings from the frailest of acquaintances, we all made our way back indoors. It was at this point that I discovered that I must have inadvertently done something which had upset my Uprights. They both sat down without even offering to feed me and then when I stood by the food cupboard and miaowed the Upright Who Smells of Oil sniffed and muttered

One of the Upright visitors seemed rather friendly.
I thought I'd try out her lap.

something about why didn't I get my new friend to feed me. Well this, of course, was just plain silly since my new friend had now gone. In the end I had to go outside and catch my own supper. By then it had started to rain and there was hardly a snack to be found anywhere. By the time I got back into the house both my Uprights had gone to bed. I was soaked, exhausted and very confused.

Love

Lemon-Coloured Lion Heart With Long Fine Whiskers

Dear Lemon-Coloured Lion Heart With Long Fine Whiskers

You're quite right of course: a new lap can make a very pleasant change. The great 16th century poet Dark Beauty of Leatheringham once wrote that 'a fresh lappe be as goode to thy soule as a rest'.

But it is clear that you inadvertently succeeded in upsetting your Uprights. And I think I know how you did this.

In order to manage Uprights successfully you have to get into their minds, to understand how they think and to know what their priorities are. Uprights will never understand us, of course, but most Uprights are very simple and it isn't too difficult to get into the mind of your Uprights and to understand what makes them tick and what makes them tock.

It is clear to me that your own Uprights are a little uncertain and lacking in confidence. They love and respect you greatly but at the moment they are uncertain of the extent of your affection for them. When you stayed on the lap of their visitor they were worried that you found her lap more satisfying than their laps. Few things worry cat loving Uprights more than the fear that another Upright has a more attractive lap. When their visitor, and your new lap, had gone home their jealousy, suppressed out of politeness to their guest, burst through.

I know that you love your Uprights but you need to show them that you love them. You need to make it clear to them that they are very special to you and to remind them that you care about them deeply.

As soon as you see your Uprights, rub your head against them.

Twine your body between their legs. Let me end with another famous quotation, this time the final lines from a famous poem by the legendary 17th century Scottish philosopher/poet Great Silken Hunter of Argyllshire: 'The cat which twineth himself twixt the legs of an Uprighte will, for heaven's own eternity, tie that Uprighte to him with bonds so steadfast none can them asunder put.'
Love
Maman

Dear Maman

For several days I have been thinking about jumping up onto the top of the television set. It's lower than the mantelpiece over the hearth (and therefore a slightly easier jump) but slightly higher than the sideboard (which is now a little too easy to present much of a challenge).
Love
Lemon-Coloured Lion Heart With Long Fine Whiskers

Dear Lemon-Coloured Lion Heart With Long Fine Whiskers

Don't be afraid to make a big leap if a big leap is required. You can't jump across a canyon, or from a fence to a tree, in two small jumps.
Love
Maman

Dear Maman

Today I plucked up the courage to try. I waited until the Uprights were both out of the room and then I jumped. And I made it. It was a wonderful feeling. I looked around the room and it was fascinating to see everything from a different angle. I was looking down on the two easy chairs and the sofa and I was, of course, higher than the sideboard. I was very proud of myself. My only regret was that you were not there to see my leap. I hope you would have been proud of me.

There was a small fly in the ointment.

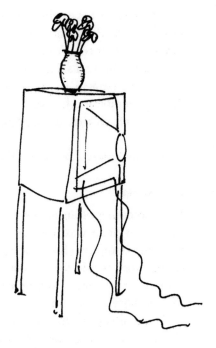

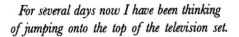

*For several days now I have been thinking
of jumping onto the top of the television set.*

When I landed on top of the television set I slid for several inches before managing to stop myself. And, since there wasn't room for both of us, a vase which had been standing on top of the television set slid off and fell to the floor where it broke into many pieces. It made quite a crashing sound, though the noise was to a small extent diminished by the water spilling out of the broken vase.

I was upset for a while but then I remembered what my friend Great White Paws had told me when describing some of his own indoor adventures: 'You can't make a jump without breaking an ornament,' he had said, adding that little unseen shrug of his with which he manages to say so much of that which remains unsaid. And, remembering his words (and the shrug), I instantly felt better and felt certain that the Uprights would understand.

Love

Lemon-Coloured Lion Heart With Long Fine Whiskers

Dear Maman

It is something of an understatement to say that the Upright Who Smells Of Soap was not pleased when she discovered the broken vase, the damp patch on the carpet and the flowers strewn around on the floor beside the television set. On reflection it seems certain that she and Great White Paws do not see eye to eye on the disposability of ornaments.

I was asleep in the spare bedroom when I heard her stamping upstairs and calling out my name. I guessed at once that she had discovered the debris and had come to an accurate conclusion about the way that the ornamental vase and the flowers it had contained had met their rather messy end and I decided that this might be a good moment to be somewhere else.

Unfortunately, I slid out of the spare bedroom at the exact moment when the Upright Who Smells of Soap arrived on the landing. She saw me, shouted something which I didn't quite catch, and started to run towards me. From the look on her face I had a pretty good idea that she wasn't intending to chuckle me under the chin so I slipped between her legs and headed straight for the stairs. I may be young but I know that when you're being chased the wisest move is to head downstairs – and for the open. (In films I've seen on television Uprights who are being chased always run upwards and invariably get trapped on a roof.)

At the top of the stairs I paused for a moment and looked behind me to see whether the Upright Who Smells of Soap was following or whether she was smiling and wanted to let me know that she wasn't really upset but that her anger had merely been for fun – much in the way that kittens pretend to be cross when play-fighting.

The Upright Who Smells of Soap wasn't smiling. Angry at the fact that I had avoided her and was now clearly about to disappear out of view she looked around for something to throw. Failing to see anything suitable she took off one of her slippers and hurled it in my direction. She missed me by a couple of yards (to be honest I think she would have probably missed if she'd thrown it at the wall in front of her), but she did succeed in knocking a porcelain statuette of a shepherdess off a window ledge six feet away from me. The shepherdess crashed onto the floor and shattered into dozens of fragments.

For some reason this angered the Upright Who Smells of Soap still further. You would have thought that since we had now broken one ornament each the Upright Who Smells of Soap would have been prepared to call it quits but, to my surprise, this wasn't the case at all. On the contrary, the destruction of the shepherdess seemed to annoy her still further and I even got the impression that she somehow blamed me for this too.

At this point she rather lost control of herself. She took off her other slipper and threw it even harder than she'd thrown the first one. I didn't wait to see what this one hit but I heard the crash as I scampered down the stairs.

Great White Paws says that if your Uprights are cross with you then you should stay out all night (or, if it's particularly cold, for as much of it as you can stand). He says that when you do finally arrive back home the Uprights will be so pleased to see you that they will have forgotten about being cross with you.

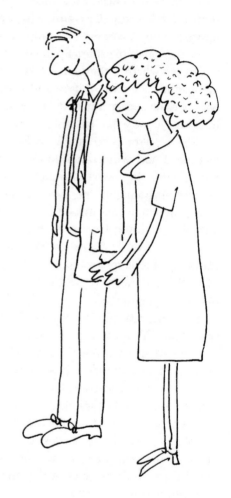

If your Uprights are cross with you then you should stay out all night.
When you finally arrive back home the Uprights will be so pleased to see you
that they will have forgotten about being cross with you.

Great White Paws' theory might work with some Uprights but it didn't work with my Uprights.

When I snuck back into the house later that evening the Upright Who Smells of Soap seemed just as cross with me as she had been several hours earlier. She chased me up the stairs, into and out of the bathroom, back down the stairs and all the way to the back door again. She then lodged something solid against my cat flap so that I couldn't get back into the house at all.

I spent the night underneath the car in the driveway. I was too cold and too frightened to sleep. A large tomcat, whose name I do not know but who often patrols our neighbourhood walked past twice. On the second occasion he smelt me and peered under the car for a moment. I held my breath and eventually he heard something which sounded more interesting than I smelt and went away.

Love

Lemon-Coloured Lion Heart With Long Fine Whiskers

Dear Maman

I was sitting on a fence this morning when next door's dog began to bark. He barked and barked and barked. At first I thought he was just in a bad mood. But then suddenly I realised that he was barking because I was there and I confess I rather enjoyed the experience. I started to walk up and down the fence, just a foot or so away from his nose. He became hysterical and barked even more. Eventually, his owner came out into the garden to see what was going on. When I saw her I sat very still and tried to look demure and innocent. The dog's owner was quite cross with him. She shouted at him a lot and made him go indoors. Minutes later I saw him looking through the patio windows. He looked very cross and was still barking.

Love

Lemon-Coloured Lion Heart With Long Fine Whiskers

Dear Lemon-Coloured Lion Heart With Long Fine Whiskers

Dogs love to make a lot of noise and to bark. It draws attention to them and makes them feel important. That's why small dogs often tend to bark more (and louder) than big dogs. It is, indeed, the thing many dogs do best. Unfortunately for dogs they tend to get told off if they bark for no very good reason.

Love

Maman

Dear Maman

Every morning the Upright Who Smells of Oil rushes around getting ready to leave the house. He has a job which he says he hates, in an office he hates, and works for a boss he hates. Every day he spends an hour travelling to work and an hour travelling home again. He says he hates the travelling too. Why does he do so many things he hates?

Love

Lemon-Coloured Lion Heart With Long Fine Whiskers

Dear Lemon-Coloured Lion Heart With Long Fine Whiskers

So much hate. So much unhappiness, frustration and distress. Uprights have addictive personalities and the substance to which they most commonly become addicted is not tobacco, cocaine or alcohol but money. Curiously, the one commodity they really yearn after is time and although they have realised that they can sell their time for money, many have not yet realised that they can also buy time with their money.

My own Upright (The Upright Who Smokes a Pipe) has worked hard all his life. And how does he get to spend all the money he works so hard to earn? He buys expensive suits so that he can impress his clients. He buys an expensive car so that he can impress his clients. He and his wife give expensive dinner parties once or twice a week, inviting people they don't like but who they believe may one day be useful to them. It makes me very sad.

Love

Maman

Dear Maman

Yesterday, I heard the Upright Who Smells of Soap say that she was having kittens today. I got very excited by this and couldn't wait to meet my new brothers and sisters. I followed her around for hours, hoping to be there at the birth of at least one kitten. But day ended, night came and there was still no sign of any kittens. Instead she had a dinner party attended by four very dull Uprights. Why did The Upright Who Smells of Soap lie? I felt disappointed and cheated. Why do Uprights lie about these simple things?

Love

Lemon-Coloured Lion Heart With Long Fine Whiskers

Dear Lemon-Coloured Lion Heart With Long Fine Whiskers

Sadly, Uprights don't always say what they mean. And they don't always mean what they say. Sometimes this is because they tell lies. But on other occasions (and this was one of them) they simply get mixed up.

Love

Maman

Dear Maman

A friend of mine says that he met a cat who said he had heard of a cat who could open doors. He said that the cat in question used to leap up into the air and dangle from the door handle until his weight opened the door. Have you ever heard of anything like it?

Love

Lemon-Coloured Lion Heart With Long Fine Whiskers

Dear Lemon-Coloured Lion Heart With Long Fine Whiskers

I have met two cats who could do this but they were never able to convince me that this sort of activity was the sort of behaviour a cat should employ. Dangling from door knobs is hardly dignified and it is not something I would like to think that a son of mine would ever do. There are two sorts of cats in this world: those who dangle from doorknobs and those who get Uprights to open doors for them.

Personally, I have always preferred to have Uprights open doors for me. It is not difficult to train Uprights to perform simple tasks such as this and I have always found that rather than regarding it as a chore they usually regard it as a privilege.

Love

Maman

Dear Maman

Something strange is happening. The Uprights have been rushing around for several days. There are boxes everywhere – in every room in the house – and the ornaments which normally sit on shelves and mantelpieces and the pictures which hang on walls have all disappeared.

Love

Lemon-Coloured Lion Heart With Long Fine Whiskers

Dear Lemon-Coloured Lion Heart With Long Fine Whiskers

It sounds to me as though your Uprights are moving home. Uprights do this quite often. The younger ones will usually move to a bigger house. When the older ones move they often move to a smaller house.

Love

Maman

Dear Maman

When I went back to the house yesterday evening, looking forward to my supper, I found that the back door had been shut. I couldn't get in. I scratched at the door, as you've told me to do, but no one answered. I then went round to the living room window, jumped up onto the window ledge and miaowed loudly. The Upright Who Smells of Oil saw me but instead of opening the window or going round to the back door to let me in he strode to the window and drew the curtains. He seemed very stern and wouldn't look at me. The Upright Who Smells of Soap who was busy putting things into a box, didn't even look up. I was hungry and feeling tired so I went

There are boxes everywhere.

to the shed at the bottom of the garden. The door was shut (as it always is) but there is a small hole at the back of the shed which I can just squeeze through. I got into the shed that way, climbed up onto a pile of old sacks, turned round three times, as you taught me to do, and went to sleep. Although I knew that there were mice around I had lost my hunger and was too upset to eat. Actually, it was a little humiliating. During the night the mice were racing around making so much noise that they woke me up once or twice.

When I woke today the sun was shining, the swallows were swooping, the flowers were open and through the shed window the garden looked beautiful; an artist would have needed a palette an acre wide to accommodate all the colours required to paint everything there. Looking around I counted more than one hundred different shades of green alone! The house was noisy and in great turmoil. Uprights in long brown coats had already started carrying boxes and furniture out to a huge van which was parked in the road outside. The van was too big to be driven into the driveway where the Upright Who Smells of Oil usually parks his car. I squeezed out of the shed and wandered cautiously over to the back door, which, unusually, had been lodged open with a piece of wood. I was hoping that someone would see me and remember that I hadn't been fed the night before.

The Upright Who Smells of Soap saw me first. She was supervising two of the Uprights in Brown Coats when she spotted me. 'Go away!' she said sharply. It was a harsh voice I didn't recognise. If I hadn't known that it was her speaking I wouldn't have believed that she would have spoken that way, or said such a thing. Thinking that perhaps she hadn't recognised me I miaowed twice, to let her know that it was me. In response, she walked over to me and, using her foot, pushed me towards the door. I couldn't believe it. I was tired (I hadn't slept very well because of the noisy mice), I was hungry (I hadn't eaten for 24 hours) and now I felt confused too.

It was obvious that I wasn't wanted in the house so I ran off down the garden, climbed my favourite apple tree (it's very low and easy to climb) and sat on one of the big branches closest to the ground. The garden no longer looked quite so beautiful. The green of the leaves, the grass and the flower stalks seemed rather muddy. The colours of the flowers, so bright before, now seemed rather dull and insipid. I closed my eyes so that no tears would roll down my cheeks and I went to sleep.

When I awoke the sun had travelled quite a distance across the sky. I stretched my front legs, yawned, stood up, shook myself and then gingerly climbed down the tree trunk. I felt ravenously hungry. I remembered Great White Paws once saying that he could eat a rat. I now knew what he meant. I headed up the garden towards the house.

Everything was very quiet when I got there. The large van that had been parked in the road had disappeared and there was, I was pleased to observe, no sign at all of the Uprights in Brown Coats.

But nor was there any sign of anyone else either.

The back door was locked again. And when I walked round to the living room window and jumped up onto the window ledge and looked inside I saw to my astonishment that the room was completely empty. All the boxes had gone. The furniture had gone. The room was entirely bare. Even the curtains had gone.

It was, I think, the moment when I saw that the curtains had gone when I realised that the Uprights must have left. And at the same moment I realised that if they had gone then they had most certainly gone without me.

Love

Lemon-Coloured Lion Heart With Long Fine Whiskers

Dear Maman

I have been taken in by my former Uprights neighbours. They seem very kind.

Love

Lemon-Coloured Lion Heart With Long Fine Whiskers

Dear Maman

I discovered today that my new Uprights have never lived with a cat before. One of them, who works in a delicatessen, smells of cheese, the other smells of aniseed. It will be quite a challenge for me but I am looking forward to the opportunity to look after inexperienced Uprights.

Love

Lemon-Coloured Lion Heart With Long Fine Whiskers

Dear Maman

Today it was raining and so, naturally, when I came into the house my paws were muddy. The Upright Who Smells of Cheese screamed when I walked across the kitchen floor and left a trail of muddy pawprints. I was so startled that I ran out again. Naturally, this meant that as I retraced my steps I produced another trail of muddy pawprints and inspired another scream.

Love

Lemon-Coloured Lion Heart With Long Fine Whiskers

Dear Maman

My friend Ebony the Hunter told me off today. She says that I make life too easy for my Uprights and that by raising my tail whenever I see them and purring whenever they make a lap available I am demeaning myself and our species. She says I should hiss and scratch a little more to keep them on their toes and to remind them of their position in the household.

Love

Lemon-Coloured Lion Heart With Long Fine Whiskers

Dear Lemon-Coloured Lion Heart With Long Fine Whiskers

There are two ways to manage Uprights. You can scratch and hiss and try to force them into doing what you want them to do because they are a little bit frightened of you and want to keep you happy. Or you can purr and treadle and rub your head against their legs and try to persuade them to do what you want them to do because they like you, they like what you do and they want you to do it even more.

Both these methods will work, of course, and the route you choose to follow must depend to a large extent upon the personality of the Upright you are dealing with. Some Uprights are stubborn and need to be pushed and bullied from behind. Some are more sensitive and respond better to kindness. A good many cats find that they can get the best results from their Uprights by combining these two approaches but I have always found that it is nearly always possible to get the best out of Uprights by being nice to them and rewarding their good behaviour appropriately. This may, of course, be because I like being stroked and cuddled. I've never understood why but some cats simply don't like being touched. Personally, I have always felt that life will be more enjoyable if you purr and raise your tail from time to time (by which I mean as often as you can, and, at the very minimum, several times a day). Cats who scratch and hiss at every slight provocation get very few cuddles.

Finally, it is worth remembering that Uprights who are treated well by their cats often live longer, healthier lives than Uprights who are treated roughly by their cats. If you like your Uprights, and they provide you with good service, then it is, of course, in your interests to keep them alive as long as possible.

Love
Maman

Dear Maman

My friend Fawn And Coffee Fur, the Silent Stalker who is embarrassed by the name his mother gave him (he says he is the worst stalker he has ever known and that he couldn't creep up on a ball of wool) and insists that I call him Plato (which is the name he was given by his first set of Uprights) says that there is no such thing as 'truth'. He says we all look at things in different ways (according to our own personal perspective) and that there cannot, therefore, be any such thing as the truth. I found this very worrying since you brought us all up to believe that the truth is very important. He says that if we both visit a place (a new stretch of woodland for example) I might find it exciting but he might describe it as dull. Neither of

us is right, he says. But we both just look at the same thing in different ways.
Love
Lemon-Coloured Lion Heart With Long Fine Whiskers

Dear Lemon-Coloured Lion Heart With Long Fine Whiskers

Please ask your friend Plato if he is really certain about what he is saying – that there is no such thing as truth.
Love
Maman
P.S. I find it sad to hear that Plato does not honour the name his mother gave him. When we mothers choose names we always select names which we think best fits our kittens. And the name Plato's mother gave him is truly beautiful. He may not consider himself to be (and may not be) a silent stalker but that was how his mother saw him.

Dear Maman

Plato says he is certain that there is no such thing as truth.
Love
Lemon-Coloured Lion Heart With Long Fine Whiskers

Dear Lemon-Coloured Lion Heart With Long Fine Whiskers

He believes that what he is saying is beyond argument? He is sure that he is not just giving you an opinion?
Love
Maman

Dear Maman

He says he is certain that there is no such thing as truth and that what he is saying is fact not opinion.
Love
Lemon-Coloured Lion Heart With Long Fine Whiskers

Dear Lemon-Coloured Lion Heart With Long Fine Whiskers

I'm afraid that Plato has proved himself wrong. He can't have it both ways.

He says that there is no such thing as the truth – and that everything we believe to be the truth is merely a point of view.

And then he says that what he says cannot be disputed – because it is the truth.

Doesn't one claim rather contradict the other?

Love

Maman

Dear Maman

Plato says he doesn't want to be my friend any more. I'm not sorry about this. He wasn't much fun to be with.

Love

Lemon-Coloured Lion Heart With Long Fine Whiskers

Dear Lemon-Coloured Lion Heart With Long Fine Whiskers

We may have difficulty finding the truth. But it's there. It may be hidden. People may not want us to find it. But it is there. And when we have found it we will know it.

Love

Maman

Dear Maman

My friend Wise Chestnut and Russet Hunter wants me to go fishing with him. I said 'yes' because I didn't like to disappoint him. But I hate fishing and I never catch anything. We have to leave the house very early in the morning and every single time I have been fishing it has poured with rain. I wish I had had the courage to say 'No' to him. I like him very much. His Uprights call him 'Toast' because they say he is the colour of perfect toast. I think they may perhaps be colour blind.

Love

Lemon-Coloured Lion Heart With Long Fine Whiskers

Dear Lemon-Coloured Lion Heart With Long Fine Whiskers

Whenever you have difficulty in saying 'No' (usually because you don't want to hurt someone's feelings) think how much harder things are likely to become (for you and for others) if you say 'yes'. Sometimes, saying 'No' is, in the long run, much kinder to everyone. Learn to say 'No' to unimportant things. Choose what you want to do. Remember that you must always say 'No' to *something*. In this case you said 'No' to staying dry and warm indoors.

Love

Maman

Dear Maman

I heard recently of a cat called Sooty who has become something of a star. He has appeared on television and has been featured widely in the newspapers. The only reason for all this attention is that he has allowed his Upright to realise that he knows what is being said to him. He has even proved that he can perform tricks and was filmed showing that he can count.

Love

Lemon-Coloured Lion Heart With Long Fine Whiskers

Dear Lemon-Coloured Lion Heart With Long Fine Whiskers

Every few years there will be a renegade cat like Sooty who, for the sake of short-term personal success and a few extra bowls of cream, threatens the very existence and survival of our species. You must never, ever allow Uprights to know that you can understand everything they say. Allow them to think that you can understand one or two words only. If they ever realise that we are as intelligent as we really are we will all be in trouble.

Love

Maman

Dear Maman

Plato says he wants to be my friend again. He and I were sitting in the living room looking out of the window. The sun was shining and the garden looked green and inviting. I suggested to Plato that we should go out and do a little sunbathing but he said we should stay indoors. 'It'll be a disappointment if we go out there,' he said. 'It'll be too hot or too windy or too dusty. And we'll have to wash thoroughly afterwards. And there will probably be dogs around.' So we stayed inside. 'The wanting is always better than the getting,' said Plato.

Love
Lemon-Coloured Lion Heart With Long Fine Whiskers

Dear Lemon-Coloured Lion Heart With Long Fine Whiskers

I felt quite depressed when I heard about your friend Plato. If we all lived our lives according to his philosophy none of us would ever do anything at all. The fact that reality might not match up to the dream you had doesn't destroy the dream. We will always have our dreams.

Love
Maman

Dear Maman

How clever are dogs?

Love
Lemon-Coloured Lion Heart With Long Fine Whiskers

Dear Lemon-Coloured Lion Heart With Long Fine Whiskers

It is my belief that some dogs can show rudimentary signs of intelligence but there is no doubt that even the most stupid cat knows far more than the cleverest dog. Dogs have very little good taste and hardly any sense. Dogs chase sticks, bouncing balls and cars (not to mention mechanical hares); they stay with Uprights who beat them and they allow their fur to be clipped and themselves exhibited as absurd examples of canine topiary. Finally, dogs bury their food in the garden and leave the stuff which should be buried lying around on the grass or the pavement.

The simple truth which you should remember always, is that when dogs and Uprights live together there is no doubt that the Upright owns the dog.

But when cats and Uprights live together there is no doubt that it is the cat who owns the Upright.

Love

Maman

Dear Maman

I really, really want to catch one of the goldfish in the pond at the house of the Upright Who Has a Large Moustache and Smells of Lager. My friend Plump Sleepy Cat Who Moves Like A Proud Eagle says the Upright Who Has a Large Moustache and Smells of Lager protects his goldfish very carefully. He says it is impossible to outwit him and catch one of his goldfish. When I asked him how he knew it was impossible he said he knew because lots of cats had tried and all had failed. When I said I didn't think that made it impossible he said that was just because I'm too young to know any better.

Love

Lemon-Coloured Lion Heart With Long Fine Whiskers

Dear Lemon-Coloured Lion Heart With Long Fine Whiskers

The impossible is only impossible because no one has done it yet. When I was a young kitten we thought it was impossible for a cat to catch a mouse in four minutes. But then Fawn Arrow did it. He spotted a mouse, stalked it and caught it in under four minutes. And then, miraculously, the barrier was broken. Now lots of cats catch mice in under four minutes. Such barriers are cat-made and they are all in the mind.

Love

Maman

Dear Maman

I caught a goldfish today from the pond belonging to the Upright

Who Has A Large Moustache And Smells of Lager. It was quite small but tasty.

Love

Lemon-Coloured Lion Heart With Long Fine Whiskers

Dear Lemon-Coloured Lion Heart With Long Fine Whiskers

I am very proud of you.

Love

Maman

Dear Maman

It's a lovely evening here, moonlit and warm and the air is full of wonderful smells. The Uprights are having a dinner party and have filled the house with noisy strangers so I thought I would find myself a nice plump mouse for supper. (I'm not entirely averse to the dinner party. I saw the chicken they were having for dinner before it was cooked and I'm confident that my meals tomorrow will consist of the usual pleasant and very satisfying mixture of skin and scrapings from the bones. But several hours of clinking glasses, loud guffaws and high pitched giggling will make sleep difficult if not downright impossible.) I have been more successful than I dared hope and at the moment I am settled on a fence post half way down the garden watching not one but three mice. And so I find myself facing a (for me) most unusual dilemma: how do I decide which mouse to choose?

Love

Lemon-Coloured Lion Heart With Long Fine Whiskers

Dear Lemon-Coloured Lion Heart With Long Fine Whiskers

Shopping for mice can be quite exhausting and for any cat in the position you're in at the moment selecting the right mouse can be quite a challenge. Choice is supposed to a good thing, but too much choice can sometimes be more of a burden than a blessing. The big danger, of course, is that you will delay making your choice for so long that all three mice will escape and you will be left empty pawed.

First, you must try to assess your chances of catching each

particular mouse. In the sort of situation you are in there is usually one mouse which will be more difficult to catch than the others. Unless that mouse looks exceptionally tasty, or the other mice look unusually unappetising, you should rule the difficult mouse out of the running straight away. Remember: your aim is to catch your supper.

Second, take a careful look at the remaining mice and try to decide which one is plumpest. By and large that is the mouse you should choose. The plumper mouse will not only taste better, and provide a more satisfying and nourishing supper, but, as a consequence of its size, it will also probably be slow off the mark and easier to catch.

Good luck!
Love
Maman

Dear Maman

Thank you, maman!
Love
Lemon-Coloured Lion Heart With Long Fine Whiskers

Dear Lemon-Coloured Lion Heart With Long Fine Whiskers

How did it go?
Love
Maman

Dear Maman

(Excuse my thinking while my mouth is full.) Everything went very well, thank you, Maman.
Love
Lemon-Coloured Lion Heart With Long Fine Whiskers

Dear Maman

Today I met my first foreign cat. It was quite an experience. Her ambitious mother, obviously knowing little of the sort of cat she would turn out to be, named her The Cat Who Will Climb The Eiffel Tower (though she is known as Fifi to her Uprights). She is a beautiful mackerel tabby with exquisite, show-winning markings, and is quite different to any cat I've ever met before. She met her Uprights in Paris where they were attached to the British Embassy (though I gather that her own upbringing was rather less illustrious) and returned to England with them when their work brought them back to London. She seems so different to every other cat I've ever met that you might almost think that she was a different species. She says she has never hunted in her life, and insists she has no interest whatsoever in an activity which she seems unembarrassed to describe as 'rude, barbaric, messy and bad for the condition of the furs'. Her Uprights have fitted a cat flap to the back door so that she can go in and out as she pleases but she hardly ever ventures outside; generally venturing out only when nature calls. She moans about this a great deal, saying that if her Uprights really understood her they would provide her with a little indoor tray so that she never had to go outside. If the weather is bad, if it is raining, for example, or if the ground is muddy, she simply won't go out at all. She confessed to me that during one five day period of unbroken bad weather she refused to go out and used the plug hole in the visitors' bathroom as a target for endeavours which might more usually have required a patch of soft earth.

She seems to me to be obsessed with her appearance. She is very conscious of her figure and, in consequence, will eat only once a day, always leaving exactly half of whatever she is given. She worries so much about her appearance that she spends every available waking moment arranging and rearranging her fur. She gets very upset if anyone (or anything) disturbs the way she has arranged things.

Love

Lemon-Coloured Lion Heart With Long Fine Whiskers

Dear Lemon-Coloured Lion Heart With Long Fine Whiskers

The first foreign cat I met also came from France and lived in the same house as myself, my sister, my Uprights and relatives of theirs who had brought her back with them.

I'm not sure whether this is still the case but in those days cats who came into Britain from abroad had to spend six months in a special isolation kennel. No one ever seemed entirely sure of the reason for this but my sister said she thought it was to make sure that foreign cats didn't bring any bad habits into the country. She said that after spending six months in isolation any cat would have forgotten all the habits she had acquired abroad.

If this was the case then the isolation period clearly wasn't long enough, for Francine (that was her name) was utterly different to all the cats anyone I knew had ever met before. Whenever my sister and I lay down, went to sleep and dreamt of chasing rabbits (our favourite way of spending every afternoon) Francine, French all the way to the tip of her immaculately coiffed tail, would parade around and around demanding, expecting and getting a great deal of entirely unwarranted attention.

You will find, as you go through life, that you will occasionally meet cats from many different countries. All exhibit slightly different characteristics. The French cats I have met have all been fussy eaters and have tended to be unfaithful and rather promiscuous. Italian cats eat too much, put on weight and wail from morning until night. American cats are invariably overweight and usually busy trying to take over someone else's garden. And German cats tend to be humourless and stout. I once exchanged thoughts with a group of friends about German cats we had all met. All of us reported that we had noticed that however early we got up in the morning we would, if there were German cats living in the neighbourhood, always find that the best sleeping position in the garden would have been already 'bagged' – particularly if it was anywhere near a pond.

Love

Maman

Dear Maman,

Today, at my third attempt, I succeeded in jumping from the sofa onto the mantelpiece. And I did it without disturbing any of the

*If there are German cats in the neighbourhood
you will always find that the best sleeping positions
in the garden will have been 'bagged'.*

ornaments. It was the biggest leap I've ever made. I was so excited that I immediately told both Dancing Like a Leaf and Raven on the Snow. I thought they would be pleased for me but Raven on the Snow was quite sniffy. 'You're being proud,' she said. 'What's wrong with that?' I asked her. 'Pride is a vice,' she said. 'Who says?' I demanded. 'My Uprights!' she replied. Is that true? Is it really sinful to be proud? I did not know how to respond to what they said. Is it bad to be proud?

Love

Lemon-Coloured Lion Heart With Long Fine Whiskers

Dear Lemon-Coloured Lion Heart With Long Fine Whiskers ,

There is a feeling common among Uprights that pride is a vice. I do not subscribe to this view which seems to me to have been devised and now perpetuated by Uprights who have nothing to be proud of and who are, consequently, determined to discourage ambition, achievement and pride in others. I firmly believe that pride, in who you are, what you do and how you do it, is a virtue. If there was more pride in the world then the world would be a much better place.

Pride is a good thing, not a bad thing. If you don't have pride in yourself, in who you are and what you do, how can you expect anyone else to have pride in you? I suspect that your friend regards pride as a sin because the Uprights do. However, I've never really understood why they do this. I rather suspect that pride became a sin because the Uprights already had seven virtues and they wanted seven sins so that the numbers matched. Eight virtues and six sins would have sounded a little self-satisfied.

Of course, too much pride can lead to disaster. My brother had a friend who was very proud of his ability to walk along very narrow branches and fences. One day, walking along a narrow tree branch, he slipped and fell. He was lucky. He fell into a fish pond and the only thing that was hurt was his pride. In his case pride came before a fall. The real tragedy, of course (as you will soon learn) is that pride is not well distributed. Many Uprights have far too much of it (far more than they should have) and the rest have far too little.

This is, I suspect, the one area where God has had more difficulty than anywhere else.

Love
Maman

Dear Maman

Early this morning I was told off for climbing onto a chair in the living room (I chose that particular chair because neither of the Uprights usually sit on it, but it is, apparently, an antique which is not to be used by anyone). About two hours later I was told off for sleeping on the carpet. This time I gather that the Upright was worried that I would leave hairs on the floor. I am trying hard to like my new Uprights. But sometimes they make me feel as though I am tolerated rather than welcomed in their home.

Love
Lemon-Coloured Lion Heart With Long Fine Whiskers

Dear Lemon-Coloured Lion Heart With Long Fine Whiskers

Thousands of years ago, cats were worshipped as gods. You should never forget this.

Never allow yourself to be humiliated.

Always retain your dignity.

And if anyone – feline or Upright – tries to take advantage of your good nature, put your paw down firmly and make it clear that you are not a cat to be trifled with.

Love
Maman

Dear Maman

The Uprights who live next door but one have a dog. They do not allow him into the house at all. Even on the coldest nights he has to sleep outside, sheltering underneath an old door which has been leant against the side of the garden shed. Almost every day the dog is beaten. I hear him whining and crying. And yet that dog is constantly faithful and obedient. If that had happened to me I would

Thousands of years ago, cats were worshipped as Gods.

have run away. But the dog stays and puts up with the punishment, the pain and the humiliation.

Love

Lemon-Coloured Lion Heart With Long Fine Whiskers

Dear Lemon-Coloured Lion Heart With Long Fine Whiskers

Dogs may have four legs, two ears and a tail but that is where the similarity to us ends. Dogs are very different to cats. A dog will be faithful to anyone, however cruel and insensitive they may be. Indeed, it is my experience that dogs show the greatest loyalty to the Uprights who treat them worst. A dog will give loyalty through fear but no cat would ever do that. A dog who is treated badly will stay with its owner and remain eternally faithful. A dog who is beaten regularly, and treated quite abominably, will still show its Upright loyalty and affection. I don't know quite why this is (though I have heard it argued by some cats that dogs, as a breed, are fundamentally masochistic). No cat would behave with such a pitiful lack of self-respect. Cats show loyalty and affection only when they feel that loyalty and affection have been properly earned. A cat who was treated badly would run away. Always remember, my dear Lemon-Coloured Lion Heart With Long Fine Whiskers, that as a cat you have a right to be treated with respect, honour, decency and affection. You have no obligation to remain with an Upright who falls down in any respect. Fortunately, most of the Uprights who agree to share their lives with cats are sensitive, caring and gentle people.

Love

Maman

Dear Maman

So far today I have been told off for going out into the garden ('You will get your paws muddy') and for coming back into the house ('You will leave pawprints everywhere'). I have been admonished for going up stairs ('I don't think it is hygienic to allow cats into the bedrooms,' said the Upright Who Smells of Cheese sternly) thrown out of the kitchen ('I don't approve of having cats in a place where food is being prepared') and physically removed from the living room after I was accused of staring at the goldfish ('You'll upset the fish if you look at them like that'). Apart from a small section of the hallway it seems that I am banned from the entire house. Since the Uprights do not approve of me going outside but have not provided me with a litter tray it is difficult to see how our relationship can thrive and prosper.

Love

Lemon-Coloured Lion Heart With Long Fine Whiskers

Dear Maman

My Uprights have asked a local animal charity to take me away. In some ways I am sad about this. I had hoped that I would be able to build up a relationship with them. The Uprights told the charity that my previous Uprights (they called them my 'owners') had had to get rid of me because of my vicious anti-social behaviour. They told the Upright from the charity that my previous 'owners' had been very patient but that I had attacked numerous people without warning or provocation and that they had to give in when I nearly blinded one of their children. (You will remember that I had scratched one of the children on the arm and the other on the leg.)

Love

Lemon-Coloured Lion Heart With Long Fine Whiskers

Dear Maman

The Upright from the animal charity is very kind. But, doubtless because of what she has been told, she is very wary. She only ever handles me when wearing thick gloves. I love being stroked but the pleasure of the experience is noticeably diminished when the hand doing the stroking is encased in a thick, rough glove.

Love

Lemon-Coloured Lion Heart With Long Fine Whiskers

Dear Maman

I am delighted to be able to tell you that I already have a new home. I don't think the people at the animal charity had very high hopes of finding me a fresh set of Uprights. On one occasion I overheard the Upright Who Wears Thick Gloves suggest to another Upright that they would probably have to arrange for me to be put to sleep. When I mentioned this to the cat living in the next cage, and added that I don't need any help in sleeping, she laughed rather nervously before telling me that when Uprights put cats to sleep they (the cats) don't usually wake up afterwards. After that I did my very best to look cute, cuddly and strokeable whenever strange Uprights came to visit. I miaowed a good deal and purred loudly when I wasn't miaowing. I made sure that I looked very meek and loveable.

Love

Lemon-Coloured Lion Heart With Long Fine Whiskers

Dear Maman

My new Uprights have a small but very neat house on a smart estate. Every room is painted magnolia, the furniture is white and the carpets are beige. I have decided to try not to go outside when the weather is bad. I think it might also be a good idea not to bring any mice into the house. Not, at least, for a while. My Uprights are called the Upright Who Smells Of Wine and the Upright Who Smells Of Gin.

Love

Lemon-Coloured Lion Heart With Long Fine Whiskers

Dear Maman

My Uprights had visitors yesterday. I had a wonderful time and was spoilt for choice. There were seven laps and it is no exaggeration to say that I would have been welcome on any of them.

This morning when I woke I suddenly felt rather ashamed of myself. I realised that my behaviour was rather self-indulgent.

Love

Lemon-Coloured Lion Heart With Long Fine Whiskers

Dear Lemon-Coloured Lion Heart With Long Fine Whiskers

I don't want ever to hear you using words like 'ashamed' again. The emotion you have described is something well known to Uprights. They call it 'guilt'. It is, I suspect, a bad habit you have picked up from them but although it sometimes occurs among kittens it is not something that should ever trouble a cat. All cats enjoy being the focus of attention. It is our duty and our responsibility. If a cat walks into a room and does not immediately dominate the attention of every Upright present he should leave immediately.
Love
Maman

Dear Maman

What should I do when I make a mistake?
Love
Lemon-Coloured Lion Heart With Long Fine Whiskers

Dear Lemon-Coloured Lion Heart With Long Fine Whiskers

Cats never make mistakes. Humans err. Cats purr. Remember that, dear Lemon-Coloured Lion Heart With Long Fine Whiskers. Repeat it every night before you go to sleep and you will have a happy life. As the great Siamese epigrammist Silver Blue Oscar once wrote: 'To err is simply human; to purr is simply divine.' Remember, Lemon-Coloured Lion Heart With Long Fine Whiskers: to err is human but to purr is feline. No matter what you've done wrong, always try to make it look like the dog did it.
Love
Maman

Dear Maman

I am so cross I cannot bear it! Two minutes ago an Upright trod on my tail and then blamed me for leaving it in his way!
Love
Lemon-Coloured Lion Heart With Long Fine Whiskers

Dear Lemon-Coloured Lion Heart With Long Fine Whiskers

Calm down my dear. Take ten big purrs.
    Love
    Maman

Dear Maman

Purr. Purr. Purr. Purr. Purr. Purr. Purr. Purr. Purr. Purr.
    Love
    Lemon-Coloured Lion Heart With Long Fine Whiskers

Dear Lemon-Coloured Lion Heart With Long Fine Whiskers

Do you feel calmer now?
    Love
    Maman

Dear Maman

Yes. I really think I do.
    Love
    Lemon-Coloured Lion Heart With Long Fine Whiskers

Dear Lemon-Coloured Lion Heart With Long Fine Whiskers

So, give silent thanks to the Upright who trod on your tail. Thanks to him you have learnt how to calm yourself when the fury within you is in danger of spilling out and damaging the world around you.
    Love
    Maman

Dear Maman

The other day I tried to eat a lizard I had caught for breakfast. It made me very ill. Strong As A Tree And Light As A Leaf laughed and said that all cats know that lizards are not good to eat. I felt very stupid.
    Love
    Lemon-Coloured Lion Heart With Long Fine Whiskers

Dear Lemon-Coloured Lion Heart With Long Fine Whiskers

The only two things you must really know are what you know and what you do not know. You should never be boastful about what you know and you need never be embarrassed about what you do not know. You learnt something valuable from your attempt to eat the lizard. You are now a wiser cat. Your friend Strong As A Tree And Light As A Leaf was wrong when he said that all cats know that lizards are not good to eat. You didn't know that, and I very much doubt if you were the only cat to be unaware of it. So, your friend Strong As A Tree And Light As A Leaf is not as clever as he thinks he is. He failed to recognise that his belief about lizards was a misconception and so he is now just as ignorant as he was before.

Incidentally, as a general rule you should never eat anything you haven't eaten before for breakfast. Always treat breakfast with great respect. And remember that if you enjoy a leisurely breakfast there is a much greater chance that the day will be a relaxed, successful and happy one.

Love

Maman

Dear Maman

My new friend Two Stars On A Black Night is very good at climbing trees. He can race up a tree in next to no time. One minute he is sitting at the bottom of the tree, looking up. The next minute he is sitting on a high branch, looking down. I would love to be able to whizz up and down trees like him. I have tried really hard but I just don't seem to be very good at it. I suppose the real problem is that although I would love to be able to climb trees like Two Stars On A Black Night can, and would love to be able to sit on branches looking down, I don't actually like climbing trees very much.

Love

Lemon-Coloured Lion Heart With Long Fine Whiskers

Dear Lemon-Coloured Lion Heart With Long Fine Whiskers

The more you enjoy something the more likely you are to become

Although I would love to be able to climb trees and sit on branches looking down, I don't actually like climbing trees very much.

good at it. If you don't like climbing trees then although you will, if you practice, be able to become competent at it you will never become *really* good at it. Some cats spend their entire lives trying to be the cat they weren't meant to be. As a result their lives are full of frustration and disappointment. Your Great Uncle is a good example. When he was a kitten his mother decided that he was going to become the world's fittest, fastest, strongest cat. She called him Mahogany With Paws as Fleet as Feathers in a Storm and spent hours forcing him to run around, climb trees and hunt down feathers blowing in the breeze. She had huge ambitions for him. But Mahogany With Paws as Fleet as Feathers in a Storm really wasn't interested in any of these things. He wasn't an athletic cat at all. On the contrary his two great loves were eating and sleeping. For the first four years of his life he tried hard to be the cat his mother wanted him to be. He hunted mice (and become tolerably good at it) and he climbed trees (and became tolerably good at that too). But his heart wasn't in it. He never enjoyed these things and so he never became the success his mother had wanted him to be. And then, when he was four, his mother became seriously ill. She called him to her side, licked him slowly and apologised to him. She confessed that she had been wrong to try and push him into a way of life that didn't suit him. 'When I've gone I want you to become the cat you've always wanted to be,' she told him. And so, when his mother passed on to the great hunting ground in the sky, Mahogany With Paws as Fleet as Feathers in a Storm gave up hunting, climbing, running and other energetic pursuits. He concentrated all his efforts on the two things he did best: eating and sleeping. And from that moment on he was not only the happiest cat on earth, he was also the most successful at what he did. He was named in several books as the world's largest cat and his Upright proudly reported that he pretty well only ever woke up when it was time to eat.

So learn to listen to your heart. Do with your life whatever makes you feel good. The chances are that if you do this then you will be both happy and successful.

Love

Maman

Dear Maman

I'm having some friends round. Is it the done thing to ask them to bring a mouse with them? Or should I provide all the mice we need?

Love
Lemon-Coloured Lion Heart With Long Fine Whiskers

Dear Lemon-Coloured Lion Heart With Long Fine Whiskers

'Bring a mouse' parties were quite popular a few years ago but these days they're rather passé except in inner city areas where some hostesses might have trouble laying their paws on enough fresh mice for a dinner party. Limit the number of guests you invite to the number of mice you are confident you can provide. You should allow between one and two mice for each guest, depending on the size of the mice and the size of the guests.

Love
Maman

Dear Maman

I went out to play but I fell into a puddle and came into the house very dirty. It took me ages to get clean again. Now I'm frightened to go out in case something similar happens again.

Love
Lemon-Coloured Lion Heart With Long Fine Whiskers

Dear Lemon-Coloured Lion Heart With Long Fine Whiskers

Your Uncle Swift As Light, Bright As Sunshine was a handsome cat (can you believe that his Uprights called him Clayborne?). He was a black and white short hair with, I think, the most beautiful markings I've seen on a cat of his type. He had lovely whiskers too. He was very proud of them.

Other cats adored him because he was patient, independent, kind, polite and full of dignity. There are few qualities which cats respect more than dignity and your Uncle Swift As Light, Bright As Sunshine had it in basketfuls. Uprights loved him because he was gentle, appreciative, very vocal and extremely physical. He loved being made a fuss of and would sit quietly on an Upright's lap for hours at a time. He was very giving too. You know how Uprights love it when a cat rubs against their legs? Your Uncle Swift As Light, Bright As Sunshine would wind in and out of their legs until they almost started purring. 'Give me five minutes with their legs and I'll have their hearts for life,' he used to say. When he was sat on a lap he wouldn't just sit there passively. He would rub his head against their arms and he would hold his head up so that they could scratch him under his chin. He loved getting lots of attention but he loved being scratched under his chin most of all.

If your Uncle had a fault it was that he was sometimes too thoughtful. He worried more than any other cat I have ever known. He worried about absolutely everything.

It was worrying too much that stopped your Uncle Swift As Light, Bright As Sunshine doing more with his life. Ever since he was a kitten he had wanted to climb trees. But ever since he was a kitten he had worried about what might go wrong. He worried about falling and being hurt. He worried about getting stuck and embarrassing his Uprights. And most of all he worried about failing – about trying to climb a tree and not being able to. He worried so much that he never once climbed a tree in his life.

The house where he lived had a garden full of trees. There were two oaks, three chestnuts and a sycamore in the front garden and an ash, a flowering cherry and two dozen fruit trees at the bottom of the garden at the back of the house. Your Uncle Swift As Light, Bright As Sunshine never climbed one of them. He wanted to. Heaven knows he wanted to. Every day of his life he would look at one of those trees and wonder what it would be like to climb it and to sit on a branch half way between the earth and the sky. But he never did. He could never quite find the courage to enable him to overcome his fears.

Your Uncle Swift As Light, Bright As Sunshine lived to be seventeen – a good age for a cat as you know – and he spent the last few years of his life regretting all those lost opportunities; those lost climbing days.

He was too old to climb by then; stiff with arthritis, a bit creaky and, to tell the truth, a little overweight. If he was indoors he would sit on a window sill, look out, admire the trees he had never climbed and wonder about what might have been and what adventures he might have had. If he was out of doors he would sit on the grass, look up and watch the branches swinging in the breeze and a tear would slowly roll down his cheek. Full of regrets at lost opportunities he would remember not the wonderful things he had done with his life (and there were many) but just the wonderful things he had never done.

Before they die all cats are expected to pass on one piece of wisdom to all the cats and kittens they know. I will never forget the advice Uncle Swift As Light, Bright As Sunshine gave to me.

'You should not be reckless or foolhardy,' he said. 'But if you don't take chances occasionally you will never know what might have happened. You will always wonder and often regret. If you protect yourself too much by never taking risks then when you get to be old you will have nothing to look back on but an endless series of missed opportunities and 'might have beens'. There won't be any point in being old. The great joy of old age is being able to look back on all the things you've done – including the mistakes.'

And so, my dear, ask yourself what is the worst that can happen if you go out to play and fall into a muddy puddle?

The worst that can happen – what Uprights call 'the bottom line' is that you will have to spend an hour or two cleaning yourself up.

Now ask yourself what will happen (not *can* happen) if you stay indoors and avoid taking that risk.

When you are old and grey and you can no longer eat two mice in a day because the second mouse gives you indigestion you will have nothing to look back on but a series of dull days when you nearly did something but didn't.

Love

Maman

Dear Maman

Chocolate Mountain laughed at me for playing. I was chasing leaves in the garden. He said I am too old.
   Love
   Lemon-Coloured Lion Heart With Long Fine Whiskers

Dear Lemon-Coloured Lion Heart With Long Fine Whiskers

Never allow anyone to make you think that you must 'grow up', or that there is anything wrong with retaining a kitten's affection for innocent fun. The world would be a much happier place if none of us grew up. What harm has a kitten ever done?
   Love
   Maman

Dear Maman

My Uprights are quite pleasant but they sometimes forget to feed me for days at a time. Today, after three days without food, I caught a mouse and brought it into the house. I did this because it was raining hard outside. As soon as they saw me both Uprights screamed. They cornered me in the kitchen and chased me out again. Sadly, I dropped the mouse before I left. I didn't like to go back for it so I then had to catch another. When I finally got back to the house I was drenched. The back door was firmly shut and no amount of miaowing would persuade them to open it for me, though I saw them both peering through the kitchen window at me. I have a feeling that my relationship with these Uprights is faltering.
   Love
   Lemon-Coloured Lion Heart With Long Fine Whiskers

Dear Maman

My Uprights have made arrangements for me to go to a new home. Last night I heard them talking about me on the telephone. My new Upright must be very keen to have me stay with him because he is collecting me tomorrow and has promised to pay my present Uprights a small sum of money, in cash, before he takes me away.

I feel that all this is my fault and that I have let you down by doing things which have clearly upset my Uprights.
Love
Lemon-Coloured Lion Heart With Long Fine Whiskers

Dear Lemon-Coloured Lion Heart With Long Fine Whiskers

If you limit your actions in life to the things that nobody can possibly find fault with, you will not do much. You have never let me down my dear.
Love
Maman

Dear Maman

My new Upright arrived this evening. He came in a small white van and was wearing long boots, a white jacket and thick gauntlets which covered his wrists as well as his hands. He smelt strongly but I had never smelt anything like it before. He picked me up from the kitchen floor and dropped me into a small metal carrying cage. He then handed my previous Uprights two small pieces of paper and shook hands with them before putting the cage into the back of his van. There were half a dozen other cages in the van. Four of them were empty. Two contained cats. 'He must love cats quite a lot,' I said to the nearest of the two cats; a fawn and white long-haired cat with tiredness in her eyes. She looked at me as if I had said something really stupid. 'Why else would he want so many cats?' I asked. The two cats both looked at me, then they looked at one another, then they looked away. They didn't say anything. Their minds are closed to me. It is as though they have put down shutters. Perhaps they know something I don't know. If they do then I wish they would tell me. Perhaps they think I will know soon enough.
Love
Lemon-Coloured Lion Heart With Long Fine Whiskers

Dear Maman

I arrived at my new home late this evening. It is unlike anything I have ever seen before. The house is not divided into rooms in the usual way but consists of a single large room which is filled with cages. Each cage contains an animal. The cages are so small that the animals confined within them cannot stand up or turn round. Many of the animals are in great pain and enormous distress. The room is filled with their cries. It smells of something I have never smelt before. Within moments of entering the room my mind is inundated with messages from cats and kittens shut in many of the cages. These are mainly warnings and cries for help and most are weak and difficult to hear, as though the animals from which the messages originate are too exhausted even to communicate clearly. One tells me that the smell is a mixture of fear and cheap disinfectant. Lots of the cats and the kittens have bandages wrapped around their heads. A good many have had their eyes removed. A number of them have tubes sticking out of their heads. It makes me weep real tears to see so many cats and kittens in such great distress. What Godless Uprights could possibly do such terrible things to such innocent creatures? I found myself wondering if I had been taken to hell.

Suddenly, the Upright who was carrying me dropped the cage I was in. He did this roughly and uncaringly and the fall, as the cage hit the floor, jolted me badly. One of my paws was trapped between the floor and the wire at the bottom of the cage and was badly bruised. It immediately started to swell and to throb. The Upright, who was wearing a thick glove on his left hand, opened my cage with his right hand and then reached in with the gloved hand and grabbed me by the neck. He pulled me out of the cage with such ferocity that I banged my head, and then literally hurled me into one of the fixed cages. As soon as I was in the cage, which was so small that I had great difficulty in turning round, he slammed the door too and dropped a metal catch into place. I was locked in. There was no water and no food. I looked up and saw that above me there was a cat in another cage. I looked down. There was a cat there too. There were cats to my right and to my left. The cages all had wire floors. The cat above me was bleeding from a savage wound on his head. Blood dripped down, through the floor of his

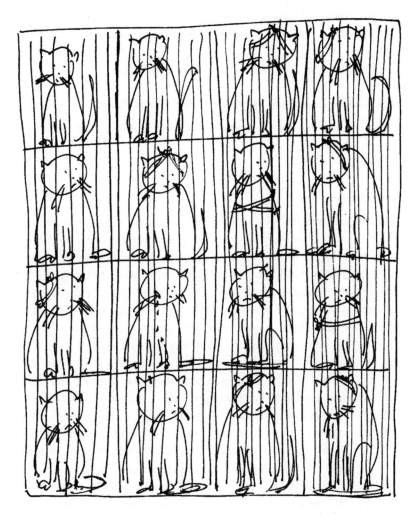

My new home is unlike anything I've ever seen before.
The house consists of a single large room which is filled with cages.

cage and onto my fur. A few drops missed me, dripped through the floor of my cage and landed on the cat in the cage below me. Moments later more fluid dripped through from above. This time it wasn't blood. It wasn't water either. I tried to shrink out of the way but the cage was too small; there was nowhere for me to hide.

Love

Lemon-Coloured Lion Heart With Long Fine Whiskers

Dear Lemon-Coloured Lion Heart With Long Fine Whiskers

I love you my darling. I pray my love will help preserve you.

Love

Maman

Dear Maman

I have been here for two weeks now. I am sorry I have not been in touch again. It is very depressing here. I have been sold to a laboratory. I have never, not even in my worst nightmare, imagined that such a place could exist. I would not even wish that dogs should endure such terror, such distress and such indignity. I don't know how many cats there are here. Hundreds at the very least. The Uprights who run this place prefer pet cats because we are easier to handle than wild ones. We are more trusting and do not scratch so readily. Some of the cats have been here for over a year. They are, not surprisingly, deeply depressed and silent for most of the time. They do not even cry. I think they have run out of miaows and tears. Some cats have had tubes put into their brains. Each day one of the Uprights comes round and pours chemicals down the tubes. The cats shriek and struggle and bang their heads against the sides of their cages. But they are unable to escape from their torment. If they could kill themselves they would. The Uprights laugh when they do this. Some of the cats have had their eyes torn out as part of an experiment. Their eye sockets, blank and bloodied stare out into space unseeing. The Uprights in White Coats sometimes taunt them by putting dishes containing food into their cages. Before the blinded cats can find the food the Uprights whisk the dishes away.

This amuses them a great deal and makes them laugh a lot. On other occasions the Uprights in White Coats will take out a cat at random, hold it by its tail and then swing it around and around. When they have done this ten or fifteen times they put the cat down on the floor and watch as it struggles to stand. This, too, makes them laugh. The Uprights in White Coats seem to enjoy their work a great deal. They all have the same smell – the same smell as the very Upright who brought me to this place. I know what it is now; it is the smell of death.

The cats who have been experimented upon, hungry and thirsty as well as frightened and in great pain, wail endlessly for days. And then, eerily, they stop wailing. They sit silently staring at the nothing they can see. The cats who, like me, are waiting to be picked out and taken into the laboratory, must simply wait in fear. There is little comfort for us.

The Uprights who work here are very cruel. They seem to enjoy their work. They are always laughing and joking. They only get upset when one of the cats they are using in an experiment manages to die and escape their clutches. That annoys them a great deal. When it happens (which is most days) they bang on our cages with metal implements and shout at us. They have a hose which they use to wash down the floors and sometimes they turn the hose on us. This makes them laugh more than ever and usually cheers them up.

The Uprights who perform the experiments are the cruellest of all and it seems from what I have been told that they too enjoy their work. The smell of death is stronger on them than on any of the others. They do not usually bother to anaesthetise us before they operate. A leather gloved assistant holds down the chosen cat, to stop it escaping or wriggling, while the vivisector wields his scalpel. Sometimes, if a cat is particularly unruly and troublesome, the scientist or his assistant will knock the animal unconscious. They do this by swinging the cat around by its tail until its head hits the wooden bench at which they are working. After the operation is over bleeding wounds are usually left to clot. Only the most severely damaged animals are bandaged; even then the dressings are

The Uprights in White Coats seem to enjoy their work a great deal.
They all have the same smell – the smell of death.

rudimentary and are hardly ever changed. Many cats develop infection but those which do are never treated with antibiotics. The lucky ones die quickly. The unlucky ones survive.

Love

Lemon-Coloured Lion Heart With Long Fine Whiskers

Dear Maman

I miss you so much, Maman. I miss you because I trust you and care for you. I miss you because you are always so kind to me. I miss you because you are always gentle and patient. I miss you because I wish I was with you. I miss you because I know that if you were here with me this would be the best place on earth for me to be. I miss you because I know that I would be happy to be anywhere if only you could be there too. I miss the gentle, caring look in your eyes, I love the warmth of your fur, I love the way you used to hold me and I miss the sweet and special sound of your purr.

Love

Lemon-Coloured Lion Heart With Long Fine Whiskers

Dear Maman

Yesterday, I learned that the Uprights in White Coats are planning to use me in an experiment. There are two types of experiment performed here. In one experiment chemicals are poured directly into our brains and the Uprights list what happens. Much of the time they get bored and simply make up the results. In the other experiments our eyes are removed. I don't know why they do this. The scientists in charge of both experiments walk round our cages once or twice a week. They carry tape recorders and large note pads with them and use them to record their observations. On one occasion one of the senior scientists was accompanied by a group of Uprights none of us had ever seen before. One of the cats who has been here much longer than I, a brave four-year-old cat whose fur is dull and knotted but whose emerald green eyes still sparkle with life, told me that the Uprights were from a Government department which was supposed to make sure that we were being well looked after and not treated cruelly. When I heard this I was filled with hope. Surely, I thought, the visiting Uprights would stop the experiments and rescue us from this hell. But they did not seem surprised or upset by anything they saw. They laughed and joked with the scientist and told him that he was doing wonderful work. One of the visiting Uprights told him that he would receive even more taxpayers' money so that he could perform more experiments. Another assured him that he could expect to be honoured by the Prime Minister and the Queen. He simpered a lot when told this and seemed especially pleased with himself.

Love

Lemon-Coloured Lion Heart With Long Fine Whiskers

Dear Maman

A few hours ago, in the middle of the darkness of the night, I was awakened when a torch was shone into my eyes. Before I could work out what was happening someone used a long, metal cutting tool to cut through the catch on the outside of my cage. Within moments I was being lifted out of the cage by a gentle Upright who was dressed all in black. Her head was covered in a black balaclava and I could see only her eyes which were blue and wet with tears. She looked frightened but kind. There were two other Uprights with her, both taller and male. They were opening the cages. After stroking me for a moment the Upright bent down and put me into a small carrying cage made of cane and wood. I thought this was a pity because it had felt good to be in the arms of a warm-hearted person who cared, but I understood. The cane and wood cage had a blanket in the bottom. The blanket was warm and soft. It smelt of dog but under the circumstances I did not mind that.

I felt confused but grateful for I was pleased to be out of that cage. I didn't know where I was being taken but I knew it must be a better place than the laboratory. I would have been happy if I had not been so full of sadness for the other cats and kittens who were, of necessity, being left behind. If I could have changed places with any one of them I would have done so.

The three Uprights in Balaclavas rescued six of us from our cages. That was all they could manage. Each of them then carried two of the cane and wood cages. They carried us out of the huge room and into a narrow dark corridor. At the end of the corridor one of them climbed through a window. The other two Uprights in Balaclavas then passed the six cages through the window before climbing through themselves.

Two minutes later, as the three Uprights were about to climb through a hole in the barbed wire fence which surrounded the laboratory, all of us were lit up by bright lights from a searchlight. There were loud, angry shouts from nearby and I heard something loud.

'They're shooting!' said the Upright who had rescued me.

'Split up and run for it!' cried one of the male Uprights, who sounded as though he was in charge.

'What do we do with the cats?' asked the other male. 'If we try to run with them we'll all be caught.'

'Take the cages through the netting and then open them,' said the leader. 'Let them go. At least they'll have a chance.'

The three friendly Uprights wriggled through the fence, pushing and dragging our cages before and behind them. When we were safely through the fence they opened our cages. For a moment I was frozen with fear. I didn't want to leave my rescuers. 'Run!' said the Upright who had rescued me. She stroked my head, then bent down and kissed me gently between my eyes.

One of the other cats, his chestnut fur blood-stained and a small, blood-soaked bandage around his head, was already out of his cage. He looked around, picked a direction, and then darted off into the blackness. 'Go!' whispered the Upright. 'Go fast! Good luck.'

As he spoke four huge Uprights in uniform appeared as if from nowhere. They wore helmets and were carrying huge sticks. A fifth Upright, a yard or two behind them, was carrying a rifle. He was overweight and I could smell that he was sweating profusely. It was sweat produced by unaccustomed exertion rather than fear. The Uprights in Uniform raised their sticks and started to attack the three Uprights who had rescued us. One of the males who had rescued us tried to run but he was shot in the back. He fell onto the grass. The other two cried out in protest and alarm as they used their arms to try to protect their heads and bodies. 'Run!' the Upright with Blue eyes shouted to me. There was desperation in her voice. There was a loud crack as one of the Uprights in Uniform hit her on the head. She fell then and it was the last thing I heard. There was nothing else I could do so I did what I had been told. I ran. For a long, long moment I was tempted to stop and return. I wanted to be with, and to comfort, the Upright With Blue Eyes who had saved me. But I knew there was nothing I could do to help her. And if I was recaptured then her risk and her pain and her courage would have all been in vain. I waited almost too long. One of the Uprights in Uniform almost caught me. But he missed me by inches, and I got away. I ran and ran and ran.

Love

Lemon-Coloured Lion Heart With Long Fine Whiskers

Dear Lemon-Coloured Lion Heart With Long Fine Whiskers

I am so relieved, my dear sweet kitten. Very few cats have ever escaped from the sort of place you've been in. I thank God (and your noble rescuers) for your liberation. They may have broken earthly laws but they have upheld God's laws.

Love

Maman

Dear Maman

When I think of the cats I left behind I cry. So many of them were so brave. The cat with green eyes I will never forget. She had the cage next to mine. Whenever I reached the depths of despair – which, I confess, was more often than it should have been – she did her best to raise my spirits. She told me that the Uprights who were working in the laboratory would, in the end, all see the light and that through our courage, dignity, patience and support for one another we would make them see that what they were doing was wrong. She told me that although we had no power, no freedom and no authority we could still reach out and touch our Uprights through our bravery and our dignity.

Love

Lemon-Coloured Lion Heart With Long Fine Whiskers

Dear Lemon-Coloured Lion Heart With Long Fine Whiskers

I am not convinced that the cat of whom you speak is right. I wish she was but I doubt if the Uprights who work in such places have the sensitivity, perspicacity or understanding to respect the innate strength and goodness of cats such as her. I hope that one day you will write your memoirs and that when you do you will refer to her. I believe that it is through speaking to a wider audience of Uprights that she, you and the rest of us can best reach out, share the truth and change things for the better.

Love

Maman

Dear Maman

In my heart I know you are right. The Uprights who worked in the laboratory did not have the minds to understand or recognise courage or, indeed, any other quality. They were driven solely by a desire to make money. I will never forget the unimaginable suffering of the cats I met in that awful place. A famous Upright, Henry David Thoreau, once wrote that it doesn't matter where you live because where you live is really in your head. To a large extent I am sure that he was right. But when he wrote that I don't think he ever imagined that Uprights could or would ever do such unforgivably cruel and wicked things to such sensitive and sentient creatures. The brave cat with green eyes told me that she believes that the Uprights Who Smell of Death will all come back as mice in their next life. It is poor consolation.

Love

Lemon-Coloured Lion Heart With Long Fine Whiskers

Dear Maman

After my escape from the laboratory I ran and walked for what seemed like an eternity.

I have been living rough in nearby woods for a while; surviving on the mice and other small creatures I can catch. Whenever an Upright approaches I run and hide. I used to enjoy the company of Uprights. Will I ever be able to trust an Upright again? I knew that some Uprights were unruly and needed to be taught the rudiments of good behaviour. But have you ever heard of such things before?

Love

Lemon-Coloured Lion Heart With Long Fine Whiskers

Dear Lemon-Coloured Lion Heart With Long Fine Whiskers

When I was a young girl, several years before you were born or, indeed, even thought of, the Uprights with whom I was living had visitors for dinner. Before the dinner started I sat in the living room and heard the Uprights talking about an Upright the visitors knew who performed experiments on kittens.

Apparently this Upright earned a very good living cutting out the eyes of kittens and then writing articles about how much they fell over when they were blind. For this work the Upright received a large grant from the Government, a generous salary from the University and additional fees from large, international drug companies.

My Uprights were initially very angry and said that there was no excuse for such cruelty but one of the visiting Uprights said the experiments were necessary because they added to human knowledge. To my horror my Uprights believed the visitor. I was so upset that I went into the kitchen and peed in the soup when no one was looking. It was surprisingly difficult because the pan was still on the stove at the time. I singed one leg quite badly. I then left that house and never went back.

I have never before told anyone about this and although I still feel a little embarrassed about peeing in the soup – it probably seems rather childish – I do think I did the right thing in leaving that house.

Love

Maman

Dear Maman

I don't think that peeing in their soup was in the slightest bit childish. I laughed at that. It was the first time I have laughed for quite a long time. I think I will make it my life's work to pee in the soup wherever I can find cruel Uprights preparing meals. What awful creatures Uprights are.

Love

Lemon-Coloured Lion Heart With Long Fine Whiskers

Dear Lemon-Coloured Lion Heart With Long Fine Whiskers

As you now know, dear Lemon-Coloured Lion Heart With Long Fine Whiskers, not all Uprights are good, kind people. Some among the species are fallen and, tragically, quite beyond redemption: thoughtless, insensitive and cruel.

There are Uprights who believe that they are the supreme beings, entitled to take and use all other creatures for their own pleasure or advantage. Some Uprights claim moral leadership of their species and believe that it is only Uprights who have souls and so it is only Uprights who merit the love of God.

This arrogant and indefensible blasphemy is used to support many obscenities and cruelties against animals of many species – including, as you have discovered, cats.

The Uprights who behave in this cruel way of death will claim that their species is entitled to subject cats to great pain and distress in ill-designed and inevitably unsuccessful experiments intended to find remedies and cures for ailments affecting Uprights.

As I have learned by simply study, this is self-serving, deceitful nonsense. The Uprights' own evidence shows that such experiments are of no value because the differences between their species and ours are so great that the results obtained from experiments performed on a cat are as irrelevant as experiments performed on an Upright would be to a cat. The Uprights continue their experiments not because they have scientific validity but because they are useful commercially.

Many experiments are performed by or on behalf of drug companies. If the results show that a new form of treatment does not kill cats then the drug will be promoted for use by humans and the company making it will say that the experiments prove that the drug is safe. If the results show that the new drug is dangerous to cats the results will be ignored on the grounds that cats are quite different to people.

Even those who support vivisection will admit that only a tiny number of vivisection experiments produce results which they can claim to be reliable. But they also admit that they don't know which experiments are reliable and which are not.

A great friend of mine, a feral cat called Dancing Moment of Joyful Warmth, has pointed out that some of the most commonly used drugs – such as aspirin and penicillin – are lethal to cats. 'If they'd tested those drugs on cats and taken notice of the results,' he said, 'doctors wouldn't have been able to use them. If the vivisectors perform 100 experiments, claim that 10 are accurate and 90 unreliable but admit that they don't know which experiments are the accurate ones and which are the unreliable ones how can they claim that *any* of their eternally damned experiments are of any value whatsoever?'

Those who defend and promote vivisection (invariably for money) have on many occasions been challenged to find one human patient – just one – whose life they can prove has been saved by animal experiments. They have never been able to do this.

Always remember, my dear, sweet Lemon-Coloured Lion Heart With Long Fine Whiskers, that these cruel and mindless Uprights are but a tiny minority. The wisest, most intelligent and best informed Uprights all regard vivisection as cruel, barbaric and pointless.

Here are quotes from just a few Uprights who disapproved of vivisection:

'Whosoever tortures animals has no soul, and the good spirit of the God is not in him. Even should he look deep inside himself, one can never trust him.'

 GOETHE

'No human being, past the thoughtless age of boyhood, will wantonly murder any creature, which holds its life by the same tenure that he does.'

HENRY DAVID THOREAU

'I know not, that by living dissections any discovery has been made by which a single malady is more easily cured.'

SAMUEL JOHNSON

'I am in favour of animal rights as well as human rights. That is the way of a whole human being.'

ABRAHAM LINCOLN

So, dear Lemon-Coloured Lion Heart With Long Fine Whiskers, I beg of you: please do not give up on Uprights. They are not all bad creatures. Many do sincerely love animals in general and are good and kind to cats in particular. A majority oppose and disapprove of the barbaric and worthless work of the vivisectors.

You will find good Uprights who will give you the love, the comfort, the privacy and the peace you deserve. Retain the faith, I beg you.

I know this, dear Lemon-Coloured Lion Heart With Long Fine Whiskers.

I know this, in my heart.

Love

Maman

Dear Maman

I know that you are right in all that you say. But I still have nightmares about the cats I left behind in that awful place. One day I would like to do something to help them.

Love

Lemon-Coloured Lion Heart With Long Fine Whiskers

Dear Lemon-Coloured Lion Heart With Long Fine Whiskers

One day you will help them. One day, my dear, you must tell your story. You must help all Uprights to understand what goes on in their name. You must encourage Uprights to stand up and fight on behalf of cats everywhere.

Love

Maman

Dear Maman

I think I have found new Uprights with whom I can live.

I was so hungry last night that I raided a dustbin behind an old house. While trying to get out of the dustbin I knocked it over. The crash brought a concerned-looking Upright out of the house. He was wearing a corduroy jacket, corduroy trousers and a pair of plimsolls. He had shoulder length hair and a long, straggly beard.

I tried to get away but I haven't eaten terribly well for quite a while and the experience at the laboratory left me weak. The Upright caught me in two strides and picked me up. I struggled, in a vain attempt to get free, and scratched his hands and wrists quite badly, but his soothing voice and soft, calm hands eventually soothed me. He invited me to his home for something to eat.

'Look what I found outside,' he told a group of Uprights in the kitchen.

'The poor thing looks as though he is starving,' said one.

They gave me a saucer of milk, a piece of cheese and some strips of chicken. I quite forgot my manners and gobbled everything down as though I was afraid someone would take it all away from me – which I confess I was.

Love

Lemon-Coloured Lion Heart With Long Fine Whiskers

Dear Lemon-Coloured Lion Heart With Long Fine Whiskers

I am so pleased and so relieved to hear that you have found new Uprights to look after. Do let me know as quickly as you can how you get on.

Love

Maman

While trying to get out of the dustbin I knocked it over.
The crash brought a concerned-looking Upright out of the house.
He was wearing a corduroy jacket and corduroy trousers
and had shoulder-length hair and a long straggly beard.

Dear Maman

The new house where I am living is occupied by six Uprights and five Little Uprights. There are also four dogs, three other cats, a hamster, a guinea pig, twelve white mice in a large cage and a tame rat which is allowed to roam freely and which the other cats tell me we are not allowed to harm.

Love

Lemon-Coloured Lion Heart With Long Fine Whiskers

Dear Maman

The other three cats have taken against me for some reason. They have been living together for four years and have decided that they do not want a young cat in the house. I think they are upset because I have been getting a lot of attention.

Love

Lemon-Coloured Lion Heart With Long Fine Whiskers

Dear Maman

The other three cats never leave me any food. Since they are the elders I wait for them to finish but when it is my turn all the food has gone. The Uprights are kind and sympathetic but they are busy and do not always notice

Love

Lemon-Coloured Lion Heart With Long Fine Whiskers

Dear Maman

Last night I was attacked and had to be taken to an Upright Who Smells of Disinfectant. I had six stitches in my thigh. My right ear was badly torn. I am very fond of the Uprights I am living with (they are kind animal lovers for whom I have great affection and respect) but I do not think I can ever be happy there.

Love

Lemon-Coloured Lion Heart With Long Fine Whiskers

Dear Maman

The Upright Who Smells of Disinfectant would not let my Uprights take me back home with them. They were sad about this but both agreed that he was right. They told the Upright Who Smells of Disinfectant that I am too gentle and not assertive enough to survive in their hectic household. The Upright Who Smells of Disinfectant is allowing me to sleep in a cage in his surgery. He told my Uprights that he will find a new home for me.

Love
Lemon-Coloured Lion Heart With Long Fine Whiskers

Dear Maman

A small grey cat who is called Whisper Of Smoke Above A Blazing Hearth occupies a cage near to mine. He has told me that the Upright Who Smells Of Disinfectant is lying. He says that the Upright Who Smells Of Disinfectant will sell me back to the vivisectors' laboratory. Whisper Of Smoke Above A Blazing Hearth has been here for two weeks convalescing after a serious operation. He says that in that time he has seen the Upright Who Smells Of Disinfectant hand half a dozen cats over to an Upright working for the laboratory. He says that if I want to survive I must escape. I have decided that when the nurse opens my cage in the morning I will leap out, run between her legs and dart out of the door into the corridor outside. From there I will take my chances. I am so frightened that I will be asleep when the nurse opens my cage – and, therefore, too slow to escape – that I am determined to stay awake all night.

Love
Lemon-Coloured Lion Heart With Long Fine Whiskers

Dear Lemon-Coloured Lion Heart With Long Fine Whiskers

I will stay awake with you.

Love
Maman

Dear Maman

Thank you. Without your love and support I do not know how I would be able to cope. I am also inspired by the courage of Whisper Of Smoke Above A Blazing Hearth. He has had a very serious operation and is clearly still extremely ill. But he has time to think of me. His courage is a fine thing.

Love

Lemon-Coloured Lion Heart With Long Fine Whiskers

Dear Lemon-Coloured Lion Heart With Long Fine Whiskers

There are many courageous cats around. Sometimes, their bravery is breathtaking. Mostly, it is inspiring.

When I was much younger I once knew a three-legged cat called Passion of Spring. She had lost one of her legs in an accident with a motor car. For six months after the accident she struggled really hard to learn to walk again. For several months all she did was go round and round in circles. She had lost her sense of balance and really found it difficult to walk again. Then, slowly, she mastered the skill she had lost. It took her time, patience, effort and courage and those who knew and loved her were full of respect for her.

But there was one cat among us who never gave her the respect she deserved. Darker Than Blackness Without Light, a young black and white cat who was very full of himself, repeatedly sneered at her efforts. He told her that if anyone ever organised a three-legged race for cats she would win it easily. His taunts upset her greatly but she didn't let him know. She just put more and more effort into learning how to get around on her three legs. First, she successfully mastered walking, then she learned how to run and finally she learned how to climb.

And then one night in summer, nearly nine months after Passion Of Spring had had her accident, a few of us got together and organised a sports meeting. The main event was a 400 yard race across four gardens. Entrants had to climb six fences, leap a stream and, at one point, climb a tree in order to jump over a wire fence.

When Passion Of Spring announced that she intended to enter

the race we were all very impressed. But Darker Than Blackness Without Light laughed and sneered and told her that she would never get over the first fence, let alone stand a chance of winning the race.

On the night of the race there were twelve entrants. We all lined up at the starting line and although we knew we would do our very best (it would be patronising to Passion Of Spring to do otherwise) we all wanted her to win. All of us except Darker Than Blackness Without Light. Naturally, he wanted to win the race himself.

It would be nice to tell you that Passion Of Spring won the race. But she didn't, I'm afraid. She had difficulty climbing over one of the fences and fell twice from the tree overhanging the wire fence. She came ninth. Darker Than Blackness Without Light, the winner, strutted around enjoying his moment, constantly reminding everyone that he had won.

But his strutting went unnoticed. None of us were much interested in his win. We were all far too impressed by Passion Of Spring's courage in finishing the course and coming ninth. It was her victory over her disability which impressed us far more than Darker Than Blackness Without Light's easy, almost painless victory in the race. His victory was memorable only for its gracelessness; her victory, her personal victory, was unforgettable.

The winning cat isn't necessarily the cat who comes first.

Love

Maman

Dear Maman

I am living wild on the streets. The trouble is that the other cats on the street are much smarter than I am. Life is, it seems, simply one darned thing after another. I have found a small shed on an allotment where I can rest.

Love

Lemon-Coloured Lion Heart With Long Fine Whiskers

Dear Maman

The owner of the shed found me this morning. I recognised her at once. It was the Upright Who Smells of Pink Roses. 'You remind me of a kitten I once knew,' she told me in a whisper. 'I fell in love with him but he could not stay with me. He already had a home.' She took me home with her.

Love

Lemon-Coloured Lion Heart With Long Fine Whiskers

Dear Maman

My Upright is every bit as kind, thoughtful and loving as I had remembered her. Living here is not the great challenge I once imagined my life would be. I will not convert her into a gentle Upright for she is already that. But she loves me, I know. And I love her too. I have experienced much in my short life – more, dare I say, than I would have chosen to experience – but life now is good.

Love

Lemon-Coloured Lion Heart With Long Fine Whiskers

Dear Lemon-Coloured Lion Heart With Long Fine Whiskers

I am so pleased that you have found a good Upright. The cat who knows that he has a good life is indeed a rich cat. Do not worry about needing more of a challenge. You have already done a great deal. And now you will, perhaps, have the time to tell the story of your ordeal at the vivisection laboratory. Your story will help educate many Uprights. And, in due course, now that you are settled, perhaps you will have kittens of your own.

Love

Maman

Dear Maman

I have never thought of that. I have always thought of myself as just a son – never as a potential father.

Love

Lemon-Coloured Lion Heart With Long Fine Whiskers

"You remind me of a kitten I once knew," she told me in a whisper. "I fell in love with him but he could not stay with me. He already had a home."
She took me home with her.

Dear Lemon-Coloured Lion Heart With Long Fine Whiskers

We all have different roles to play in our lives. To you I am a mother. But to my brother I am a sister and to my own mother I am a daughter. I think of myself as a mother but I also like to think of myself as something of a philosopher. When I was younger I was, so cats have told me, quite attractive. I was the fastest runner I knew and a good enough fighter to have put several belligerent tomcats to flight. So, you see, you have many roles to play. To me you will always be a beloved son. But to others you will be many other things.

Love

Maman

Dear Maman

The older I get the more I realise that I want to do something to help change the world. There are so many battles to be fought. How can I possibly fight them all?

Love

Lemon-Coloured Lion Heart With Long Fine Whiskers

Dear Lemon-Coloured Lion Heart With Long Fine Whiskers

When I was pregnant with your older sister Snow Flake Who Dances On The Wind I wandered out into the garden one night for a walk. (I always have trouble sleeping when I'm pregnant.) It was a beautiful, cloudless night and the moon was very nearly full. The sky was a beautiful dark blue, decorated with a million stars, and the air was clear and warm. It was one of those perfect nights which, sadly, most of us never know anything about because we spend them asleep, curled up in our baskets or on our cushions, quite oblivious to the wonder above and around us.

I had gone no more than a couple of dozen yards from the back door when I suddenly found myself face to face with a fox.

Now, before that night I had only ever seen a fox from a distance but I knew at once what the creature was. He seemed as startled to see me as I was to see him. He was young, plump, well fed and in wonderful condition. His tail was bushy and full.

Both unmoving, we stared at one another for what seemed like an hour, though I don't suppose it was more than a minute or so. And then, without either of us making a sound, we simultaneously turned and retraced our steps.

Was it in the fox's nature to walk away like that? I suspect not. I think he would normally have attacked me.

So, why didn't we fight?

Was it fear?

Maybe.

He could see that I was pregnant and would know that I would be fighting for at least two. But I don't think a fox will often walk away from a fight with a cat.

Was it respect?

Perhaps.

When we looked at each we both had respect for one another. But respect does not usually stop a fox.

I think it was the wonder of the night which somehow affected us both. We were both at one with our worlds that night but we both realised that the worlds we were in were the same world. It was not a night to die.

The fox might have been able to kill me but I would have probably been able to do him a considerable amount of damage. Maybe he would have died too. And what would we have been fighting for?

Choose your battles with care, my child. Walk away from the battles which are of no importance. But fight the battles which matter to you with all of your heart.

Love

Maman

Dear Maman

Do you remember that poem you always used to tell us when we were small?

Love

Lemon-Coloured Lion Heart With Long Fine Whiskers

Dear Lemon-Coloured Lion Heart With Long Fine Whiskers

The one called simply 'Cats'?
>Love
>*Maman*

Dear Maman

Yes, that's the one. Tell it to me again, please Maman.
>Love
>*Lemon-Coloured Lion Heart With Long Fine Whiskers*

Dear Lemon-Coloured Lion Heart With Long Fine Whiskers

>Cats are always happy
>Except when they are sad
>Cats are always good
>Except when they are bad
>Cats are always hungry
>Except when they are fed
>Cats are always cuddly
>From their tails up to their heads
>Cats are all adorable
>Every single one
>Cats are all remembered
>Even when they're gone
>Love
>*Maman*

Dear Maman

That always used to make my cry when I was a kitten. But way back then I didn't know why it made my cry. It still makes me cry. But now I know why.
>Love
>*Lemon-Coloured Lion Heart With Long Fine Whiskers*

Cats are all adorable.
Every single one.

For a catalogue of Vernon Coleman's books
please write to:

Publishing House
Trinity Place
Barnstaple
Devon EX32 9HG
England

Telephone   01271 328892
Fax   01271 328768

Outside the UK:
Telephone   +44 1271 328892
Fax   +44 1271 328768

Or visit our website: www.vernoncoleman.com